Segmenting
the Industrial
Market

Segmenting the Industrial Market

Thomas V. Bonoma
Benson P. Shapiro
Harvard University

LexingtonBooks
D.C. Heath and Company
Lexington, Massachusetts
Toronto

Library of Congress Cataloging in Publication Data

Bonoma, Thomas V.
   Segmenting the industrial market.

   Bibliography: p.
   Includes index.
   1. Industrial marketing. 2. Market segmentation. I. Shapiro, Benson
P. II. Title.
HF5415.B525 1983   658.8   82-49325
ISBN 0-669-06578-1 (alk. paper)
ISBN 0-669-09469-2 (pbk.: alk. paper)

Copyright © 1983 by D.C. Heath and Company

Fourth printing, September 1984

Published simultaneously in Canada

Printed in the United States of America on acid-free paper

Casebound International Standard Book Number: 0-669-06578-1

Paperbound International Standard Book Number: 0-669-09469-2

Library of Congress Catalog Card Number: 82-49325

To Emil and Marie Bonoma, Kenton and Florence McElhattan, Ernest and Rose Shapiro, and Sidney and Rose Weinstock, who have provided us with valuable traditions, loving guidance, and unwavering support

Contents

Figures and Tables

Figures

Tables

Preface and Acknowledgments

The evolution of this work was guided by two principles. The first was the notion of interlocking segmentation nests themselves, which came to us from observing managers in the best companies and from our own consulting attempts to make sense of industrial markets. The second was our deep belief that no aspect of the selling process, including segmentation, can be separated from how the customer buys. Therefore we required that our segmentation scheme incorporate what is known about organizational buying. We believe the result is powerful and of utility both to managers and academics.

Many people contributed materially to this book, although we remain solely responsible for any errors in it. At the Harvard Business School (HBS), E.R. Corey served admirably in dual roles as the project's mentor and, as director of HBS research activities, facilitator. At the Marketing Science Institute, which provided funds, encouragement, and substantive help with our revisions, we thank Alden Clayton and Diane Schmalensee. Kathy Jocz's superb editing made a real difference in the final book.

During the core development itself, still others were helpful. Professor Theodore Levitt of HBS, Associate Dean Frederick Webster of the Amos Tuck School at Dartmouth, and Professor Ray Corey read several of the interim drafts and graciously shared with us their comments and criticisms. Professors Rowland Moriarty and Barbara Jackson, also of Harvard, willingly shared some of their concepts and ideas about segmentation. Yvonne Greene and some others, including Rose Giacobbe and the word-processing staff at HBS, bore the brunt of trying to read our writing and convert it into sensible prose. And Elaine Bonoma took on the arduous task of preparing the index and proofreading the typeset manuscript.

Finally, it is not only traditional but necessary in this instance to thank our wives, Elaine Bonoma and Norma Shapiro, for the support, encouragement, and real help that they bring to every activity in which we engage. Like good management, their impact is not easily quantifiable but makes large bottom-line differences.

1 Introduction

The complexity of industrial markets, products, and usage systems makes it critical for marketers to understand market structure and dynamics. Careful, astute market segmentation can save a marketing executive a great deal of time and money by helping to prevent false starts, inefficient marketing programs, and poor performance. Industrial market segmentation clearly is not the total answer to effective marketplace performance, but it is a necessary, and often critical, component of theory and practice. It is a practical, useful tool for industrial marketing executives.

Defining Segmentation

Segmentation is the process of separating a market into groups of customers, prospective customers (prospects), or buying situations such that the members of each resulting group are more like the other members of that group than like members of other segments. Market segmentation can be viewed either as a process of aggregating individual customers, prospects, and buying situations into groups or as a process of disaggregating a total market into pieces. In either case, the aggregation-disaggregation process can go through many or only a few stages; one can disaggregate a market into segments and then further disaggregate each segment into subsegments, and so forth.

In general, there are many possible ways to segment any market. For example, the separation of a market into different customer groups might occur around companies, people, or other parts of the purchase. The best way to segment a market will depend upon the purpose of the segmentation process. There are three major reasons to segment a market:

1. Analysis: To understand better the total marketplace as well as how and why customers buy.

1

2. Market selection: To choose for marketing attention those segments that best fit the company's competence.
3. Marketing management: To facilitate the development of strategies, plans, and programs to meet profitably the needs of different segments, as well as to provide the company with a distinctive competitive advantage.

Every good marketing executive would agree that "you have to know the territory." The marketer must understand in depth the customers who are being approached, the ways in which they buy, and the reasons they pursue the products they do. Because all customers and all purchase situations are not the same, one cannot consider the market as a homogeneous entity. One also cannot make plans and policies based on an average customer or an average purchase. On the other hand, usually it is not possible to analyze each customer and each situation separately. The solution is to segment the market into homogeneous subgroups. Once such segments are isolated, the marketer can study each of them carefully, circumventing the need to study each individual customer or situation. In one sense, the process of segmentation itself is part of the analysis. Companies, people, or situations are grouped until it is possible to understand the differences between and similarities among them.

One purpose of this market-analysis process is to help the marketer to select some parts of the market for attention and (in all likelihood) to disregard other parts. If segmentation is done well, marketers can make intelligent choices about the fit between their company and products and the needs of each segment. Those segments that fit the company's capabilities are chosen for penetration. Those segments that do not suit the company's capabilities are left for others to serve (Corey 1975).

Segmentation can also serve as a basis for developing strategies, plans, and programs that profitably meet customer needs. Clearly if needs, purchasing processes, and other key characteristics differ among market segments, different strategies are needed to approach each group. The more varied the needs and the more complex the buying process, the more important it is to segment the market.

Analysis, market selection, and marketing management all require market segmentation. Thus segmentation is at the core of good industrial marketing. Conversely, many industrial marketing problems stem from poor market segmentation.

Growing Need for Industrial Market Segmentation

In a classic article written almost thirty years ago, Wendell R. Smith (1956) discussed the nature of market segmentation as compared to another marketing approach, product differentiation. He pointed out that there is an ebb and flow to marketing strategy over time. When starting out with a new product or in a new industry, marketers attempt to devise programs which will "bring about the convergence of individual market demands for a variety of products upon a single or limited offering to the market" (p. 4). In this strategy, which Smith labeled product differentiation, the marketer appeals to superior or unique "product claims designed to make a satisfactory volume of demand *converge* upon the product or product line being promoted" (p. 4).

As competition intensifies, other vendors enter with similar products, and production technology becomes more sophisticated, allowing smaller economical batch sizes to be produced, Smith felt that marketers could begin to turn away from differentiation as a strategy. "The marketer may determine that it is better to accept *divergent* demand as a market characteristic and to adjust product lines and market strategy accordingly. . . . The strategy of product differentiation here gives way to marketing programs based upon measurement and definition of market differences" (p. 4). (It is perhaps unfortunate that Smith chose these terms, particularly *product differentiation,* since they later developed meanings substantially different from his apparent intent.)

Smith painted this movement from product differentiation to market segmentation as an evolutionary development showing increasing sophistication in marketing. In the years that have passed since he wrote, all of the emergent conditions he cited as a reason to segment have become daily facts of life to marketers. Competition in any market worth having is especially intense today. Even the highest barriers to entry do not seem to allow the firm to dominate a market for very long before similar products are introduced. Customers are ever more diverse and more demanding of specialized products to meet their unique needs. Segmentation, like product differentiation, has become a necessary practice for the industrial marketer. As Smith would put it, the question today is whether to attempt to serve the whole market with a "promotional strategy . . . concerned with the bending of demand to the will of supply" or with market segmentation, a "merchandising strategy, merchandising being used here in its technical sense as representing the adjustment of market offerings to consumer or user requirements" (p. 6).

Previous Work in Industrial Market Segmentation

In August 1978 the *Journal of Marketing Research* published a special section, "Market Segmentation Research." The editor, Yoram Wind of the Wharton School at the University of Pennsylvania, is an expert on organizational buying behavior and market segmentation. Yet even a scholar of his stature and interests had not one article to include in the special section that dealt in more than a passing manner with industrial market segmentation. The reason is that very little academic work has been done on industrial market segmentation.

A careful search of the literature shows that only a few articles have had any direct, important impact upon the development of industrial market segmentation. If the marketing practitioner's requirements for pragmatism and relevance are taken into account, the deficiency is even greater. In fact, a great deal of the work that does exist on market segmentation is not directly applicable by the practitioner but rather is concerned with the development of basic theory or new methods. In the special issue, Wind devoted only one-half page of a seventeen-page article to "translating segmentation findings into strategy." The section began: "The most difficult aspect of any segmentation project is the translation, and, in fact, little is known (in the published literature) on how this translation occurs" (Wind 1978, p. 333).

Industrial marketing practitioners have not been active in filling the void left by academics. Wind and Cardozo studied industrial marketers' reports of how they were segmenting their markets and concluded that although segmentation obviously was taking place, it was not necessarily either explicit or well reasoned. They found, "Industrial marketers do differentiate their marketing programs among customers. But the differentiation appears less a conscious, explicit strategy of market segmentation, and more an explanation or concept applied *after* the fact to explain differences in the success of particular marketing programs" (Wind and Cardozo 1974, p. 160).

Purpose and Nature of This Book

The need for good approaches to industrial market segmentation is clear and growing. But the literature on industrial market segmentation is sparse at best and the literature on applications of such segmentation in general almost nonexistent. Furthermore, industrial marketers generally may not have applied clear or explicit market-segmentation strategies. This book is designed to address this situation and thus help fill the need for a better approach to industrial market segmentation. The intent is to provide a scheme useful to researchers desirous of rethinking and extending what is known about market segmentation and to provide practitioners with several tools to execute better the segmentation task.

The remainder of this book is divided into three major sections. Chapter 2 provides an explanation of a new, nested approach to market segmentation. We believe the scheme is useful both as a conceptual framework for organizing past research and as a guide for practitioners. One of the primary thrusts of this approach is that there are many ways to segment a market and the best way to do so depends upon the specific situation.

Chapters 3 through 7 reorganize the existing literature on market segmentation, as well as the literature on industrial buying behavior useful for segmentation purposes, in terms of the segmentation nests conceptual framework. Chapter 3 reviews the outermost nest of demographic segmentation variables, which may be examined by the marketer. These include the familiar geographic, Standard Industrial Classification Code, and other macrosegmentation tools. Operating variables, covered in chapter 4, represent a generally new approach suggested by the nested concept. Chapter 5 reviews what is known about the purchasing practices of the buying company and how the company uses the goods it procures. Factors such as buyer-seller relations and the way in which the buying company approaches the purchasing task are looked at as segmentation variables. Situational factors, such as the application to which a purchase will be put or the risk level entailed in the purchase, are reviewed in chapter 6. Finally, chapter 7 reorganizes and simplifies the previous literature devoted to understanding the nature, psychology, and dynamics of the individual buyer as a corporate player and fits these approaches into the nested scheme. In these chapters, the intent is not to review all of the available literature but only that which seemed to have clear implications for industrial segmentation from our perspective.

Chapters 8 and 9 represent the third major part of the book. If the nested-segmentation approach is to be useful for marketing practitioners, it is necessary to investigate how managers can implement it. This is the topic of chapter 8. One of the major concerns regarding implementation must be monitoring and control. Chapter 9 is an excursion into marketing controllership with a focus on segmentation.

Thus the book provides

1. A new way of thinking about segmentation;
2. A reorganization of what is known about each relevant segmentation level, and
3. An implementation and control guide to aid in installing and monitoring the industrial firm's segmentation scheme.

There are two strategies readers may adopt to allocate their time. Those who have neither the time nor inclination to review the empirical work we cover in chapters 3 through 7 may wish to read only the core of what we offer. They should read chapter 2, which presents our nested approach, and chapters 8 and 9, which tell how to apply and control it. For most readers, however, we believe that there is real benefit in a careful examination of chapters 3 through 7 in the proper sequence, for each contains insights and generalizations not captured in the more-general exposition.

2

A Nested Approach to Industrial Market Segmentation

There are many ways to segment industrial markets. Sometimes several ways seem appropriate, and at other times none may seem useful. In some cases, there seems to be no differentiating characteristic among a company's customers that can serve as a basis for splitting them into groups. One able consultant recently said to us, "There seems to be no basis on which to segment this market. My client has 15 percent of the market for this type of equipment, but there is no unifying theme to its customer mix or to anyone else's." The frustration was justified and understandable, but it was no reason to give up. At least the consultant knew that 15 percent of the market has purchased one brand. That in itself is one basis for segmentation. Potential segments do exist, even if the only apparent basis for segmentation is previous brand choice.

At other times, the marketer is baffled by the array of segmentation options that suggest themselves from even a casual inspection of the market. Customer demographics, including industry and company size, operating characteristics (production technology is an example), purchasing organization and culture, and the personal characteristics of the buyers all may differentiate customer groups. Usually the market splits obtained from analyzing different variables may all differ as well, that is, customers, prospects, and purchase situations group in different ways depending upon the variable used to segment. The problem is to know which, and how many, of the possible bases to use and how to interpret the differences in the results. Identifying the relevant segmentation bases and knowing how many to employ to segment the market are the concerns of this chapter.

Given a belief in the usefulness of segmentation for shaping marketing strategy, a central question is what dimensions are appropriate for segmentation purposes. We have identified five general segmentation bases:

1. Demographics,
2. Operating variables,

3. Purchasing approach,
4. Situational factors, and
5. Personal characteristics.

In order, these proceed from general, easily observably characteristics about industries and companies to specific, subtle, hard-to-
assess bases. In the nested approach to segmentation, the marketer
moves from the outer nests containing the more general, easily observable potential segmentation bases to the inner nests with the
more-specific subtle ones (figure 2-1). It may not be necessary or
even desirable for every industrial marketer to go through every stage
of the nested approach for every product. It is also possible to skip
irrelevant nests. It is important, however, for readers to understand
the approach completely before making decisions about the best
level of the nest at which to stop.

Demographics

At the outermost level are demographics, or variables that give a
broad description of the company. Paramount among these are:

1. Industry,
2. Company size, and
3. Location.

All of these variables relate in some sense to customer needs and
usage patterns. They can be ascertained externally without entering
the prospective customer's premises.

Industry is important because it provides a general understanding
of the needs of the customer and its way of looking at purchase
situations. Some companies, such as those that sell paper, office
equipment, or business-oriented computers, market to a wide range
of customer industries. For these companies, industry is an important
basis for segmentation. Hospitals, for example, share certain computer needs and differ as a group from, say, retail stores.

Sometimes it is important to determine at what level of specificity the industry should be divided. For example, one could consider financial services as a single related industry. But commercial

banks, insurance companies, stock-brokerage houses, and savings-and-loan associations differ dramatically from each other in terms of product and service needs. For example, if one sold computers to financial services companies as a market, their different requirements for specialized peripherals and terminals, data handling, and software would soon show the need for a more-detailed segmentation scheme.

Company size has a great impact on market segmentation. It might be, for example, that a small supplier of industrial chemicals segments its prospective customers on the basis of size, choosing not to service large customers because their volume needs are beyond the scale of the supplier's capacity.

The third demographic characteristic is location. Location is a particularly important segmentation variable in decisions related to sales deployment and organization. A manufacturer of heavy-duty pumps for the petrochemical industry would want to provide good sales coverage to the Gulf Coast because of the concentration of customers there, while putting perhaps only little effort into New England. Location is also important in situations where proximity to the customer is a requirement for doing business, such as in marketing products of low value per unit weight or volume (corrugated boxes or prestressed concrete) or where personal service is critical (job-shop printing).

All of these variables can be ascertained externally to the customer. Directories, either industry oriented or general, can be used to develop lists of customers by industry, size, and location. Government statistics and privately developed reports available from market-research houses, industry publications, and trade associations can provide a great deal of data arranged around these variables.

Segmentation based on the outer nest in figure 2-1, the demographic variables, is similar to what have been called macrosegmentation approaches in the marketing literature. Broad, externally observable, often industry-wide characteristics of potential customers have been recommended as a way to segment industrial markets. Recently, though, some writers have maintained that such an approach is by definition only partially accurate for any one potential customer and have advocated using microsegmentation variables like the personal characteristics of buying decision makers to segment markets (Choffray and Lilien 1979). We believe there are several additional levels of analysis between macroanalysis and microanalysis that can be useful to the marketer.

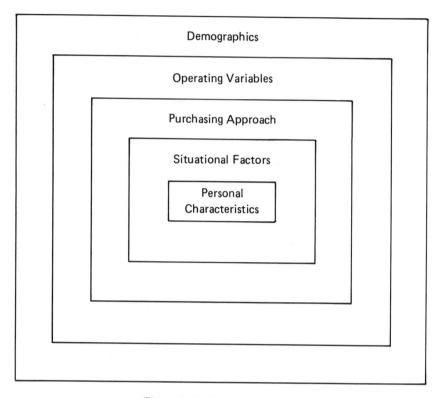

Figure 2-1. Nested Approach

Operating Variables

Somewhat less general than demographics are a variety of segmentation bases that we call *operating variables*. Most of them can be used to separate prospects and customers within a general industry category. These variables include the following:

1. Technology
2. User-nonuser status
    a. Product
    b. Brand
3. Customer capabilities
    a. Operating
    b. Technical
    c. Financial

The prospect company's technology, related to either its manufacturing process or the product planned, will have a great deal to do with its buying needs. Color televisions, for example, are produced in Japan in highly automated fashion using a few large integrated circuits. In the United States they are produced using many discrete components, with manual assembly and fine tuning. In Europe, production techniques involve a hybrid of integrated circuit and discrete components. The television-production technology has a great impact on the kind of test gear, tooling, and components in which the customer will be interested.

One of the easiest ways, and in some situations apparently the only obvious way, to segment a market is by product and brand use. Users of a particular product or brand generally have some characteristics in common that have made them users. At the very least, they have some common experience with a product or brand. Because this is such a clear-cut way to segment a market, the user-nonuser dimension deserves a closer look.

Manufacturers that have chosen to replace metal gears with nylon gears in a particular piece of capital equipment probably share perceptions of nylon and metal, the way they respond to risk, their manufacturing process or cost structure, their marketing strategy, or some other aspect of their company. Perhaps they have been subjected to a similar sales presentation about nylon gears. Once having produced some machinery with nylon gears, the executives of the companies have some common experience and some similarity in their manufacturing approach. A new supplier of nylon gears might reason that companies that have already made a commitment to the generic-product category will be better prospects than those that have not yet done so. Another new supplier might reason, in the opposite way, that manufacturers that have not yet shifted to nylon will be easier prospects because they have not experienced the benefits of nylon and have not yet developed a working relationship with a nylon-gear supplier.

The same type of thinking can be applied to brand choice. Current customers can be viewed as a segment differing from people using the generic product but purchasing it from someone else. A supplier's current customers are familiar with its products and services, and the supplier knows something about the customer's needs and purchasing approaches. Some companies explicitly develop marketing approaches that separate the amount of additional sales volume they want to generate from existing customers (either from customer growth or from gaining a larger share of the customer's business) and the additional sales volume they desire from new customers.

Sometimes it is useful for a company to segment customers not only on the basis of whether they buy from it or from one of its competitors but also, if the latter is the case, from which competitor they purchase. This information can be used in several ways. For example, some competitors might be weaker than others, at least in some respects. The idea then is to concentrate on the customers of the weak competitors.

In some industries, suppliers can be placed into subgroups that approach the market in the same general manner. Thus, of seven suppliers, three might compete for the high-quality, intensive-service part of the market and four for the high-volume, normal-service part of the market. Assuming that customers served by a particular subgroup have common needs, a company might tend to go more aggressively after the customers of a competitor in the same subgroup than in the other subgroup.

Another approach related to brand involves implicit (and apparently legal) coalitions between suppliers. If one company supplies only the top-quality part of a product line, another company that offers only the lower-quality part might reasonably attempt to obtain the low-quality business from the high-quality supplier's customers. Together the two companies have formed a coalition capable of supplying all of a customer's needs.[1]

The third aspect of operating variables involves the customer or prospect company's capabilities. Companies with particular operating, technical, or financial strengths and weaknesses might make especially appropriate customers. For example, companies that operate particularly well with tight raw-material inventory might be especially appropriate for a supplier with an unusually reliable delivery record. Regarding lack of operating competence, customers not capable of performing quality-control tests on incoming raw materials might be willing to pay more for supplier checks regarding quality. Some vendors have been particularly astute in identifying customers needing technical support and in providing it in a highly effective manner. In the reverse situation, Digital Equipment Corporation for many years sold its minicomputers to sophisticated customers able to develop their own software. Because of differences in financial strength, some companies are more attracted by leasing and vendor-financing packages than others. Some suppliers, because of what they believe to be a more-sophisticated credit-control process, will accept customers that other companies turn down and charge higher margins to justify the added risk taking and extra service. Segmentation for market-selection purposes is one of the most important uses of segmentation.

To some extent the operating variables are visible from outside the company. A quick drive around a soda ash plant, for example, might tell a vendor salesperson the type of technology being used by the plant. Financial strength is, at least to some extent, available from credit-rating services such as Dun & Bradstreet. Other data, such as the name of the current supplier, may have to be gathered from customer personnel. Information obtained by techniques such as reverse engineering (tear down or disassembly) of a product to find the type and sometimes producers of components or noting the names on trucks delivering goods to prospective customers can supplement conversations held with executives of the prospect firm.

Figure 2–1 shows that a subsequent nest, the next to innermost, involves situational factors. Situational factors are more temporary and require a more intimate knowledge of the customer or prospect than operating variables. Operating variables, including vendors and brand choice, tend to be somewhat stable. It is unusual for industrial purchasers to make frequent changes among vendors other than rotating among a continuing set of vendors who occupy the company's "short list," or regularly used, purchasing sources.

Purchasing Approaches

One of the most-important yet neglected bases for segmenting a market involves the purchasing approach and philosophy of a company. This nest includes variables such as:

1. Formal organization of the purchasing function,
2. Power structure,
3. Nature of existing organizational relationships,
4. General purchasing policies, and
5. Purchasing criteria.

The data necessary at this level must by and large be gathered directly from the personnel of the customer or prospect. As we begin to consider these variables, we will also note a relationship in some situations between them and others.

The organization of the purchasing function is related to both size and mode of operation of the purchasing organization. Centralization (Corey 1978a, chapter 4; Corey 1978b) has the effect of merging individual purchasing units into a single larger one; thus it plays some of the same role as size. If units that are organizationally centralized are dispersed geographically, the varible takes on some of the characteristics of location as well. For example, a source company that operates only regionally may not be able to supply all of the locations of the centralized customer. Or companies with decentralized manufacturing operations may find it difficult to conform organizationally to centralized customers' buying patterns.

Power structures in customer companies differ with regard to the relative influence of various functions. When powerful engineering personnel exert a good deal of influence in purchasing situations, technically skilled suppliers have a competitive advantage. Other companies have influential financial units. Many observers believe that the strong financial-analysis units at General Motors and Ford have led to a price orientation in their purchasing decisions. While the impact of these functions varies among specific purchase decisions, they often exert strong effects on the purchasing approach.

A third variable in this category involves relationships. At the most-mundane level, it might be possible to identify a set of customers with which a sales manager has a stronger than normal relationship. This type of link might also be broader than the user-nonuser variable. An investment banker might, for example, define as one unattractive market segment all companies on whose board sits a representative of a competitor. Sometimes these relationships are traditional; the concept of a customer totally loyal to one supplier because of a long and fruitful history of doing business together is relevant here.

General purchasing policies and tendencies can be important. A financially strong company that offers a lease program might attempt to identify a segment of prospects oriented toward leasing capital equipment or at least toward meticulous asset management. Other relevant prospect tendencies might be the desire to do business with long-established companies, a stress on affirmative-action programs in purchasing (relevant to minority-owned businesses and their competitors), the desire to do business with small independent companies, or an interest in buying systems instead of individual pieces.

Also included under general purchasing policy is the prospective customer's approach to price negotiations. Some companies tend to negotiate an agreement based on supplier costs, as is often the case with the auto companies and the three large general-merchandise chains (Sears, Ward's, and Penney's). Others negotiate from a market-based price, and still others use bids (Corey 1978a). Because bidding puts so much emphasis on price, some vendors that have cost advantages might identify companies that choose suppliers by bidding as a desirable segment, while other vendors might make the opposite choice.

The last three variables—power structure, nature of relationship, and general purchasing policies—are important because of their impact on purchasing criteria. The criteria used to make purchase choices and some of the situational variables seem to lend themselves to something akin to benefit segmentation in the consumer-goods market—that is, the process of segmenting a market around the reason the customer buys (Haley 1968). Benefit segmentation is, in fact, the most-powerful form of segmentation (although not always the most useful) because it deals directly with customer needs. Purchasing criteria can be an important segmentation variable even in situations where a marketer cannot seem to find a more-basic reason for the criteria used.

A great deal is known about several of the purchasing-approach variables. For a number of years, marketing scholars have studied the internal organization of the various buying groups or decision makers in industrial companies. A good deal of study has also been done on the nature and types of salesperson-buyer relationships.

Situational Factors

So far the discussion generally has been framed in terms of segments that are composed of individual customers, either companies or people. At this point, we consider segments that may be composed of individual purchase situations and even single line entries on the order form. Before doing so, however, we have to look more closely at what is perhaps the most-basic approach to segmentation: benefit segmentation. Haley (1968) identified the benefits desired by different prospective customers as the fundamental way in which to segment a market. The benefits might be simple or complex, product related or related to the service support so important in the industrial marketplace. Thus benefit segmentation is the identification of groups of prospects and customers especially interested in a particular benefit.

Some benefits relate to the company as a whole and to persons within the company; others are situation specific and relate to individual orders. Among those situational factors are:

1. Urgency,
2. Specific application,
3. Size of order, and
4. Size of a particular part of an order.

Urgency has proved to be a useful segmentation variable in many industries where a product can be needed either in regular use or in emergency replacement of an existing part. Some companies have found urgency of need a useful way to segment a market for market selection or for developing a focused marketing-manufacturing approach.

A supplier of heavy-duty stainless-steel pipe fittings might define its market as the fast-order replacement market. Thus, when a chemical plant or paper mill needs to replace a fitting, it will look to this company only if its need is urgent. At that point, the vendor's application engineering, flexible manufacturing capacity, and installation skills will be worth a premium price. In the general procurement of routine replacement parts, on the other hand, the vendor cannot justify its premium price. Here the segmentation is order based; is it an order needed right away?

Product application is another basic situational factor. Application will have a great effect on a computer purchase. For example, certain computer companies emphasize business applications; others emphasize technical applications. The segmentation in that industry can reach as far as very specific applications. Technical applications divide into areas, such as computation and simulation. The particular application can have a major impact on the purchase process, purchase criteria, and thus the vendor chosen.

Segmentation can and should go down even further to the individual line entry on an order form. A company with highly automated equipment might segment the market such that it targets only those specific items on a customer's order for which the unit volume ordered is large and for which the vendor can benefit from the low variable cost of its automated equipment. A nonautomated company, on the other hand, might want only the small-quantity short runs on the order form. In this situation, the respective vendors would have to convince the customer to divide its overall order into two orders, one long run and one short run, if they were to be successful in implementing their marketing-segmentation concept. In many industries, such as paper product and pipe fittings, a primary function of distributors is to take the overall orders and to purchase the long runs from one vendor and the short runs from another. This is a particularly good example of the process of both disaggregation (splitting an order) and aggregation (combining orders).

At the level of the nest, attention is focused on the situational variables involving a particular purchase decision and on an individual order or part of an order. Here the company looks at uses as well as users of its products. The distinction is an important one because many users have different suppliers for different specific uses. The pipe-fittings manufacturer that responds only to urgency is a good example.

Situational factors can have a large impact on the previous nest level, purchasing approaches. At General Motors, for example, a clear distinction in purchasing process and organization is made between product purchases (purchases of raw materials or components for a product being produced) and nonproduct purchases. The urgency variable is so powerful that it changes the purchase process and criteria; an urgent replacement is generally purchased on availability, not price.

The interaction between the situational-factors and purchasing-approaches nests is a clear example of the permeability of the divisions between nests. Industry, a variable in the outermost demographic nest, helps to determine application, a variable in the situational-factors nest, although industry by no means totally determines the application.

Little is known in the literature about situational factors. Although practitioners sometimes segment to the level of a line item on orders (electrical distributors are a good example), academics generally have not extended their segmentation inquiries in this direction.

Personal Characteristics of Decision Makers

Purchasing decisions are made by people, not by companies. The people may work in an organizational framework and be constrained by company policies and needs, but they remain people. Accordingly markets can be segmented at the level of the individuals involved in a purchase, using many of the same methods applied for consumer products.[2] We will simply illustrate a few of the more-important points here because there are so many potential approaches.

Among the variables in this nest are buyer-seller similarity, buyer motivation, individual perceptions, and risk management strategies. Some buyers are risk averse and some risk prone. The level of risk a buyer is willing to undertake seems to be related to other personality variables, such as cognitive style, intolerance for ambiguity, and self-confidence (Cox 1967). For example, it has been found that the amount of attention a purchasing agent will pay to cost factors depends on the uncertainty about the decision, as well as whether credit or blame for the consequences will accrue to the agent. Those buyers who are risk averse tend not to be good prospects for new products and new concepts. Risk-averse buyers also tend to shy away from trying untested vendors.

Some purchasers are meticulous in the way they objectively approach the buying decision; they shop around, look at a number of vendors, and then split their order for assured supply. Others tend to rely on old friends and past relationships and seldom make comparisons among vendors. Some are especially vulnerable to bribes and near-bribes.[3] All of these and many other variables represent meaningful ways to segment a market.

Understanding and Applying the Nested Approach

Industrial marketing executives have a wide range of alternative segmentation approaches available. The most-relevent ones often relate directly to customers' desired benefits and the vendor's skills, but at various times other approaches to segmentation make more sense. Sometimes order or individual line entries on an order are more useful for segmenting a market than are customer characteristics. Further, the nests are not independent of one another, unrelated, or impermeable to entry of factors in other nests.

As the nests go from the outside to the inside, as shown in figure 2-1, the variables considered change in terms of visibility, permanence, and intimacy. That is, the factors in the outer nests are generally highly visible even to an outsider, are fairly permanent, and require a much-less-intimate knowledge of the prospect or customer. Both the fourth nest (situational factors) and the fifth nest (personal characteristics) are of low visibility, are temporary, and require quite intimate vendor intelligence. Which one should be the innermost nest is still debatable. Situational factors change with each new situation, but situations tend to repeat themselves in the marketplace. Individuals do not change their characteristics, but positions in an organization are populated by different people at different times.

A natural question is, "Where do I stop as I move through the nest?" The short answer is, "As soon as you find a useful approach." The complete answer, however, must be a bit more detailed. We suggest that generally a manager begin at the outer edge of figure 2-1 and work toward the center. Although the levels do not form a hierarchy, it is easier to begin at the outside and work inward. In some situations, however, because of prior knowledge and work, an executive would begin at a middle point and work inward or perhaps (but less probably) work outward.

The first step in the process is a mental one. It consists of carefully thinking about segmentation and the nested approach. We recommend that the manager or, even better, several managers mentally work their way completely through the nest. After a while it will become clear that some methods of segmentation are likely to yield greater benefits than others and that some methods cannot even be considered without better data. The purpose of the segmentation will determine the appropriate level of effort to expend in the process and the general way to approach it. A warning is necessary here: at this stage, one should not decide that an approach is not useful because data are not available. The nested process requires an independent assessment of analytical promise and data availability. The two steps should not be confused.

When the necessary data are gathered, the managers can make an intelligent assessment of several approaches. Wherever possible the outer nests should be chosen over the inner nests because the outer ones are easier to work with. On the other hand, the situational and personal variables of the innermost nests are often the most useful and powerful. In our experience the situational level is certainly the most-neglected approach toward segmentation.

We suggest two simple yet useful diagrammatic approaches to applying the nested-segmentation scheme. First is the two-dimensional matrix or chart. In many situations, a market can be segmented along several dimensions that interact with one another in important ways. An example will help to explain. The fabricator of specialty stainless-steel pipe fittings, who offers speedy fast service at premium prices, developed the matrix shown in Figure 2–2 for use in planning its marketing strategy. The pipe manufacturer initially decided that it would attempt to meet only the high-urgency needs (the horizontal dimension); it then decided to serve the large customers directly and to use distributors to reach the small ones. Further analysis showed, however, that distributors often stocked smaller fittings used by both large and small companies, while large fittings were used only by large customers and were not available from stock. At this point it became clear that another chart would be more useful (figure 2–3). This process of analysis led the company to devote its efforts to satisfying the urgent needs of large companies that use large fittings.

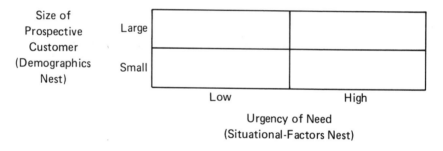

Figure 2-2. Segmenting by Size of Customer and Urgency of Need

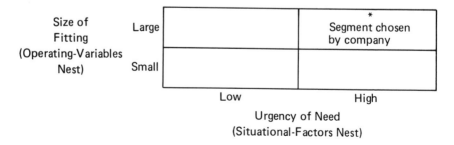

Figure 2-3. Segmenting by Size of Fitting and Urgency of Need

Profits increased significantly because the sales force could focus on one type of customer (large), and the production and physical-distribution function could focus on one type of order (urgent).

These two-dimensional spaces, maps, matrixes, or diagrams are extremely useful. It is important to understand that an executive might want to develop several different diagrams with different nest variables and test each for relevance. Because there are many different ways to segment a market and several valid purposes for segmentation, it takes a few attempts to identify the most-useful diagram. Note that the variables used in the pipe manufacturer's pair of two-dimensional matrices involved three different nests. This is a further indication of the interactive and permeable nature of various nest levels. The useful application of the nests depends upon the creativity, knowledge, and judgment of the user.

The second form of diagram that we have found to be of use is related directly to the market-selection process. It gives a manager a way to record on one chart the importance of a variety of different benefits to a number of market segments and the ability of several competitors to meet these needs. In the first step, the executive lists the various benefits of importance to different customers (or purchase situations) in the industry and uses these to label the rows of a chart (see figure 2-4). The columns are related to different market

Benefits and needs	Competitors and Segments			
	Segment A	Segment B	Competitor 1	Competitor 2
Custom design		*	*	
Delivery reliability	*			*
Fast delivery	*		*	
Product line breadth	*		*	
Quality		*		*
Price				

Figure 2-4. Market-Selection Diagram

segments. In the second step, the manager analyzes the strengths of various competitors, including the executive's own company. A system of importance weights (1 to 5, A to D, or symbols such as stars and pluses) is then placed in the boxes, indicating the importance of that benefit to the market segments or the ability of a competitor to provide the benefit. In our example, market segment A places high value on reliability of delivery, fast delivery, and breadth of choice and low priority on custom design, quality, and cost. Competitor 1 can provide custom design, fast delivery, and product line breadth, while competitor 2 specializes in reliability of delivery and quality.

Part of the strength of this chart arises from the fact that it includes benefits, segments, and competitors. Once the chart has been completed, an executive can scan it fairly quickly to identify the fit between his or her own company and competitors on the one hand, and market segments on the other. It can help the executive make plans to do one of the following: change the market segments that the company is attempting to capture, change the benefits the company is offering, or attempt to persuade a given market segment(s) that the benefits that the company can provide are the most-important or relevant ones. The value of this approach is that it aids executives in discussing key issues at a high level of specificity rather than in philosophical generalities.

Summary

The nested approach has five basic messages:

1. There are many ways to segment a market.
2. It is difficult to choose among the many ways.
3. The choice can be made only after a great deal of analysis and a great many attempts, some of which will end in success and some in failure.
4. It is often best to use more than one segmentation approach.
5. The elegance of a segmentation scheme is not related in any way to its usefulness.

In general it is better to test mentally many approaches and reject most of them than not to test them at all. Judgment must be applied in segmentation. Situational factors will often predominate to the point where generalities will be too simple to be useful.

At first glance the nest may not be easy to understand. It is based, however, on the concept that three factors influence the purchase process: the company (its demographics, operating variables, and purchasing approach), situational factors, and personal characteristics of the individuals involved in the purchasing process. The purchase process in turn leads to the purchase decision. Figure 2–5 outlines the relationships.

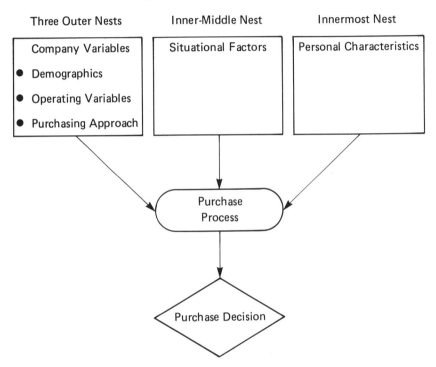

Figure 2–5. Another View of the Nests

3

The Outer Nest: Demographics

Demographics is the most frequently employed basis for industrial market segmentation. Using company-level variables, marketers attempt to identify homogeneous market subgroups. These variables usually are of the type that do not require access to the prospect's premises; they are externally observable. Perhaps the most frequently employed demographic variables are industry, location, and size. Each of these variables is available for scrutiny to the marketing manager. For current customers, they can be extracted from company records.

Industry

The combination of government and commercial data sources allows reasonably complete specification of prospects by industry. The government originally developed the *Standard Industrial Classification Manual* to generate statistics to describe the national economy. All economic activity is included in the SIC system and is separated into classes that are asigned code numbers. Figure 3–1 provides a concise explanation of the four-digit SIC system used in the manual.

Every five years, the Census Bureau, using an expanded seven-digit SIC code system, classifies industrial output more precisely. For any product classification within an industry, the number of companies manufacturing the product or delivering the service is recorded. The total quantity of the item produced is compiled, as is its manufactured value. Industry shipments are recorded, including both domestic and export units and dollar values. The result is that the *Census of Manufactures* provides a static but relatively complete picture of products and industries every five years.

In theory, the manufacturer wishing to identify new market opportunities could simply assess the SIC codes of current customers buying heavy volume, obtain a state-government directory of business for the market area of interest, and select from the directory all

A. The Standard Industrial Classification System

Division	Industries Classified	Major Industry Groups
A	Agriculture, Forestry, and Fishing	01, 02, 07, 08, 09
B	Mining	10-14
C	Construction	15-17
D	Manufacturing	20-39
E	Transportation, Communications, Electric, Gas, and Sanitary Services	40-49
F	Wholesale Trade	50-51
G	Retail Trade	52-59
H	Finance, Insurance, and Real Estate	60-67
I	Services	70, 72-73, 75-76, 78-86, 88-89
J	Public Administration	91-97
K	Nonclassifiable Establishments	99

B. Breakdown of the Standard Industrial Classification System

Classification	SIC Number	Description
Division	D	Manufacturing
Major Group	34	Manufacturers of Fabricated Metal Products
Industry Subgroup	344	Manufacturers of Fabricated Structural Metal Products
Detailed Industry	3441	Manufacturers of Fabricated Structural Steel
Manufactured Products	34411	Manufacturers of Fabricated Structural Metal for Buildings
Manufactured Products	3441121	Manufacturers of Fabricated Structural Metal for Buildings—Iron and Steel (for sale to companies): Industrial

Source: Adapted from Haas (1976, pp. 36-38), based on Office of Management and Budget, *1972 Standard Industrial Classification Manual* (Washington, D.C.: U.S. Government Printing Office, 1972); U.S. Bureau of the Census, *Census of Manufactures, 1967 Industry Services: Fabricated Structural Metal Products* (Washington, D.C.: U.S. Government Printing Office, 1970).

Note: The U.S. economy is divided into eleven divisions, including one for nonclassifiable establishments. Within each division, major industry groups are classified by two-digit numbers. Part A illustrates the basis of the SIC system, showing the eleven divisions and the major industry groups within each division. For example, all manufacturing firms are in division D, and two-digit numbers from 20 to 39 indicate major manufacturing industries. SIC 22 includes all manufacturers of textile-mill products, SIC 25 includes all manufacturers of furniture and fixtures, and SIC 37 includes all manufacturers of transportation equipment. The two-digit SIC numbers describe major or basic industries. Within each major two-digit SIC industry group, industry subgroups are defined by a third digit, and detailed industries are defined by a fourth digit. This is the basis of the four-digit SIC system found in the *Standard Industrial Classification Manual:* the longer the number, the more detailed the industry being defined. It is also possible to supplement the four-digit SIC numbers with five-and seven-digit SIC numbers provided by the *Census of Manufactures.* An example of this appears in part B. The seven-digit SIC numbers are very specific, and the use of the seven-digit numbers provides good industrial-market-segmentation criteria. For example, SIC 344112 defines fabricated structural metal for buildings—iron and steel for sale to other industrial companies. SIC 3441125 defines the same products but for sale to commercial, residential, and institutional customers. In this case, the seven-digit SIC numbers provide market-segmentation data not available through the use of the four-digit SIC numbers provided by the *Standard Industrial Classification Manual.*

Figure 3–1. Standard Industrial Classification Code

firms not currently customers that fall in served SIC codes. As Hill, Alexander, and Cross (1976, pp. 131–146) have pointed out, however, there are some difficulties with using data classified by SIC code for market-segmentation purposes. The classification system makes two assumptions that its own data show are dubious. The first is that all establishments placed in the same code classifications engage in the same kinds of activities. For some industry classifications, like steel mills, this assumption largely may be correct. For others, such as the retail-trade categories, the specialization ratio computed by the *Census* may show that less than 60 percent of the total output of the businesses in a given classification is devoted to the product defining the category.

The second assumption is that "establishments belonging to a given category account for a large proportion of the total activity included in that category" (Hill, Alexander, and Cross 1976, p. 136). Clearly this coverage ratio is likely to be higher for some categories than for other categories. The point is that the SIC-based classifications give readily available measures of industry type to the marketer only at the risk of oversimplifying a set of very complex relationships.

Although the SIC system has been the target of a good deal of just criticism regarding its construction and usefulness, it is nonetheless true that "a practical classification system for industrial customers already exists, and firms in practically every industry in the United States are already classified by appropriate SIC numbers. If the marketing manager knows enough about present and potential customers to classify them to at least four-digit SIC market segments, that manager is halfway home" (Haas, 1976, p. 37).

Commercial vendors of SIC-compatible data, such as *Sales and Marketing Management's Survey of Industrial Buying Behavior,* have attempted to improve on some of the shortcomings in the Census data. SMM's *Survey* allows managers to perform relatively sophisticated segment planning and market-coverage calculations. Table 3-1 gives an example of the SMM data.

Location and Size

Location and size, along with industry, are important determinants of usage patterns and customer needs. Both variables need to be considered and defined carefully. For example, the term *location* can refer to purchasing location, receiving location, or usage location. For some purposes one form of location will be much more important than the others. An executive performing a logistics study or a transportation-profitability analysis, for example, would consider receiving location, not purchasing or usage location, and a service executive deploying a force of repair people would need to know the usage location of the product. The sales force, obviously, would concentrate on purchasing locations. (Logistics and service are part of the marketing strategy and in some industries could be major determinants in the analysis of markets, the selection of prospects and customers, and the development of marketing approaches.)

At this nest level, size refers to size of a company. For some other purposes, though, one might prefer to think about the size of an individual plant, store, or other receiving or usage site; the size of an individual operating unit or profit center (such as division); or the size of the total entity. The nature of the purchase process can have a strong impact on apparent size. Centralized purchasing, for example, can make individual-customer operating units into one big customer. Note that we are not considering here the size of an individual order.

Size, like location, has an impact on profitability and servicing and can be important in market analysis, selection, and planning. Some companies, for example, make a conscious decision to encourage smaller customers because such customers do not have the leverage to exact price and service concessions. Other companies concentrate on larger accounts because they generate more dollars of sales per dollar of sales expenses. Still others pursue both markets but use a different approach to each. In still other instances, smaller customers are handled by distributors, and larger ones are serviced on a direct basis.

Assessment

Outside of government and trade publications, little to no academic attention has been devoted to analyzing or improving macrosegmentation tactics. Although the available demographic variables of company location, size, and industry do appear to meet the dual criteria of being easily identifiable and of splitting the market into homogeneous groups, it is not at all clear that such variables alone always lead to increased profits or better marketing. Wind and Cardozo (1974), for example, found that demographic variables were most often used by marketing practitioners because of their low cost, acceptance by others in the firm, and clear identification of customers. But neither Wind and Cardozo nor anyone else has evidence that macrosegmentation alone repays its cost to the firm employing it.

Thus there is a large gap in the academic and business literature concerning implementation issues. At what point does it become cost-ineffective to split the market into smaller and smaller industry groups? What level of market disaggregation leads to maximum profits? We hope to clarify these issues in chapter 8.

The demographics level of the nest is usually the easiest to use because the data are easily available, the classifications fairly straightforward, and the concepts generally accepted among practitioners. A wealth of data is available, most of it from public sources. Although there are problems of overgeneralization and misclassification, the data bases available provide a starting point for any segmentation effort.

Table 3-1
Example of Sales and Marketing Management 1981 Survey, County-by-County Totals for Alabama

County SIC	Metro Area Industry	Number of Plants		Total Shipments ($Mil.)	Percentage of U.S. Shipments	Percentage in Large Plants[a]
		Total Plants	Large Plants			
Autauga	180 All mfg.	23	11	192.3	0.0111	100
Baldwin	177 All mfg.	34	9	234.6	0.0136	60
Barbour	All mfg.	26	11	150.0	0.0087	68
Bibb	All mfg.	14	5	76.5	0.0044	71
Blount	All mfg.	8	4	77.5	0.0045	83
Bullock	All mfg.	5	5	70.5	0.0041	100
Butler	All mfg.	23	11	208.6	0.0121	67
Calhoun	All mfg.	65	28	633.2	0.0366	81
2281	15 Yarn spinning mills, except wool	3	3	57.0	1.2904	100
Chambers	All mfg.	15	11	349.8	0.0202	97
2211	Cotton-weaving mills	6	6	182.8	3.4857	100
Cherokee	All mfg.	9	5	48.5	0.0028	79
Chilton	All mfg.	9	5	59.0	0.0034	80
Choctaw	All mfg.	10	5	363.8	0.0211	97
Clarke	All mfg.	16	8	250.7	0.0145	68
Clay	All mfg.	13	7	132.4	0.0077	68
Cloburne	All mfg.	6	4	57.4	0.0033	95
Coffee	All mfg.	22	9	203.1	0.0118	73
Colbert	90 All mfg.	42	15	1,731.0	0.1002	96
3334	Primary aluminum	1	1	245.2	3.7333	100
3353	Aluminum sheet, plate and foil	1	1	1,021.9	12.1272	100
3361	Aluminum foundries	2	2	99.5	2.9119	100
Conecuh	All mfg.	7	3	48.8	0.0028	71
Cooza	All mfg.	9	3	49.8	0.0029	51
Covington	All mfg.	25	13	268.2	0.0155	83
2321	Men's and boys' shirts and nightwear	3	3	58.8	1.5953	100
Cronshaw	All mfg.	12	3	98.8	0.0057	69

Cullman	All mfg.	28	15	374.8	0.0217	87
Dela	All mfg.	17	6	295.1	0.0171	80
30011	Tires and inner tubes	1	1	147.1	1.4385	100
Dallas	All mfg.	37	16	468.6	0.0271	79
De Kalb	All mfg.	44	19	208.5	0.0121	79
2252	Hosiery nec	16	4	34.1	3.3540	52

Source: Reprinted by permission from *Sales and Marketing Management*'s "Survey of Industrial Buying Power," April 27, 1981, pp. 38–39. Copyright 1981.

Note: SIC Industry: classification by plant's primary product; nec: not elsewhere classified; metro area code: metro market that country belongs to; total plants: twenty or more employees; large plants: 100 or more employees; all mfg.: totals for all plants with twenty or more employees in county; shipments: dollar value of all goods produced.

aIf the share is 99.5 percent or more, it shows as 100 percent.

4

The Outer-Middle Nest: Operating Variables

The second nest level is that of the prospect's operating variables, defined as production technology used, whether the prospect currently is a user or nonuser of the product category or the vendor's brand, and the customer's technical, financial, or operations expertise. Perhaps not surprisingly, there is no evidence from academic work on any variables in this category. Academics simply have not studied this intermediate nest, preferring instead to work with purchasing approach and personal variables. Yet a careful analysis of how customers differ on the operating level can often provide a solid, workable segmentation scheme that does not need to address the more-intimate, inner nests.

Technology

There is no experimental or survey-based literature on segmentation by technology. Case research, however, shows the value of segmenting on technology in a number of industries. We look at two examples: coal mines and one part of the computer market.

There are approximately 2,900 coal-mining companies in this country. The majority of tonnage comes from surface or strip-mining applications (60 percent of all coal produced), as opposed to underground-coal mining (40 percent), done largely east of the Mississippi. Above-ground mining operations are much alike and require heavy earth-moving equipment not dissimilar to that used in highway construction. In underground mining, however, three different mining technologies are in use. Traditional mining, which uses a drill to make holes for dynamite, a cutter machine to undercut the coal face, and loading devices to remove the blasted coal, is dying out as a production method in all but very small "doghole" mines. Continuous mining, which uses a continuous mining machine to rip the coal from the face and convey it to trackless shuttle cars, accounts for most of the underground coal production. Longwall mining, which uses a

600-foot chain-driven ripper to gouge coal out along a long face, is rapidly gaining in popularity because of cost economies.

This brief description shows that the market for coal-mining equipment and supplies is actually a collection of four or five different markets. Self-contained underground rescue gear is of interest to only the eastern underground mines. Hydraulic cylinders, on the other hand, are components of both above- and below-ground mining equipment, and cylinder rebuilders might find customers in all of these markets. In this example, the technology defines the market for some products but not for others. Demographics alone, however, probably would not provide the richness of data needed for analysis, selection, and plan development.

To take a less-obvious example, consider high-technology companies competing in the computer aided design–computer aided manufacturing (CAD-CAM) market. Of the competitors in this field, several are design-and-build manufacturers, mostly making their own computers, graphics work stations, and even peripherals such as printer-plotters. Others are essentially assemblers, having proprietary software and perhaps one piece of proprietary hardware but largely using other vendors' peripherals and equipment. Study of the SIC code or other demographics will not reveal to the vendor of computer cabling which company is which. Yet companies in the former class may be heavy buyers of cabling and companies in the latter, light.

There are probably several useful typologies of technology awaiting discovery. Clearly one dimension is that of backward integration, or how much of its components and raw materials the company itself makes versus how much it buys. On closer investigation, other variables will likely turn out to be equally useful.

User-Nonuser of Product and Brand

One important operating nest segmentation variable would be whether companies used or did not currently use products in the same class as those marketed by the vendors. A similar logic might obtain for groups of users segmented by their brand choices.

Before looking at some case evidence and the sparse material on source loyalty, it will be useful to provide a conceptual framework for analyzing this particular variable. In chapter 8 we will discuss different internal and external uses of segmentation. At this point, it will suffice to point out that three major uses of segmentation inside the company are planning, forecasting, and budgeting. The user-nonuser variable is particularly good for developing an orderly approach to the forecasting of or planning for future sales growth.

Figure 4–1 shows the basic structure. Increased sales can come from either existing customers or new customers. New customers can come from getting companies in existing markets to become customers or from entering new markets, where *market* can be defined in a wide variety of ways, including geography, industry, and application.

Increased sales from existing customers can come from the customer's growth in use of existing applications. In cases where a customer increases its purchases from a given vendor in proportion to its increased use of the product, the vendor's penetration, or share of the customer's business, does not increase, although the absolute unit sales volume does. The vendor can also increase its share of the customer's business and, if the customer's total purchases stay the

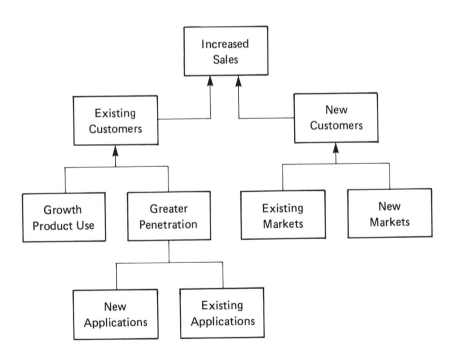

Figure 4–1. User-New User Segmentation Scheme

same or increase, its unit sales volume increases as well. One way it can do so is simply by capturing a larger share of the customer's existing purchases for current applications. Such an increase must, of course, come at the expense of other vendors. Alternatively, the customer might be persuaded to use the selling-company's product in a new application. In such a case, the competition for the new applications is not only other vendors of that product but the vendors of other products that can be used for the same applications.

The approach shown in figure 4–1 helps marketing planners to be specific in their plans and forecasts and thus adds an element of realism to the planning process. This kind of analysis can be made at a more-specific level than user-nonuser of one's product or brand. For example, a company can segment its prospects by their use of different competing products if it seems that one segment may be easier to convert than another.

The survey literature is silent on these issues, though some evidence is obtained from case examples. For instance, one critical segmentation variable in the business-jet market is whether the corporation in question uses or does not now use turboprop or better equipment. Nonowners have a buying cycle three to four times as long as owners. Their buying deliberations are radically different because there is ordinarily no corporate flight department or chief pilot who can be influenced by vendor efforts and who in turn can influence the firm's chief executive. Interestingly, a good way to identify good prospects in this nonowner segment is to look at the makeup of the board of directors. When several of the board members come from companies that do operate jet aircraft, vendors have found the likelihood of a sale to be much higher than when the board members are not in this category. This factor falls somewhere between an operating variable and a purchasing-approach variable.

The brand user-nonuser differentiation is critical to companies that market capital equipment and the spare parts, repair services, and supplies that go with them. In some situations, the parts can only be obtained from the original equipment manufacturer (OEM) so that the customers who purchase the capital equipment become a captive market for the parts. In other industries, parts and supplies are interchangeable between or among OEMs. In still other industries, such as those marketing frequently replaced parts for crawler tractors, independent suppliers (in this case called *will-fitters*) compete for the parts business. The importance of brand as a segmentation variable will differ in these three situations. It will also differ among the customers of different suppliers. The customers of some suppliers are likely to be more brand loyal in their add-on or cascaded-demand purchases of parts, accessories, supplies, and service than those of other suppliers.

Current supplier also becomes important in cases where the customers tend to become locked in to the original vendor because of high costs of changing vendors. The costs might involve additional training of operators and mechanics as in the case of aircraft-navigation equipment, duplication of spare-parts inventories as in the case of aircraft or aircraft engines, incompatible software as in the case of business or technical computers, or incompatible equipment interfaces as in a data communications system. The added costs might be actual or potential. Many IBM customers continue to buy IBM equipment because of a fear of incompatibility in software or hardware. The risk of change or disruption in itself can be a substantial cost and thus a good reason to remain loyal to a given vendor.

The material on source loyalty in the next chapter is related closely to the user-nonuser variable. Some types of customers in some situations are more loyal than others. A market-selection dilemma is presented: it is clearly incumbent upon the vendor to attempt to attract the loyal customer because of its longevity, but the nonloyal customer is easier to attract. An argument can be made for stressing either the loyal or the nonloyal customers. We cannot make any useful generalizations except to say that the situation as well as the customer type must be considered.

Purchase of Related Products

Just as there is a competitive side to products and brands, there are also complementary relationships among products in the marketplace. Take the parts and service for capital equipment. Certainly a parts seller for bulldozers would segment the market for both market-selection and program-development purposes based upon a prospect's ownership of bulldozers. It would be important, for example, to know how many bulldozers were owned and what models they were. Those data, along with product activity (such as hours per day used), would provide a good estimate of parts usage and thus of sales potential.

The product relationships can be more subtle. In the consumer market, the purchase of film follows a well-known and predictable pattern after the purchase of a camera. In the first year, film purchase is very high on average. It declines each year, until use is very low by about the fourth year. We believe that there is a similar timing issue in some industrial markets. The purchase of parts and supplies could, in many cases, be related (perhaps inversely) to the original purchase date of equipment. Prospects in many situations could be more likely to buy accessories and other add-ons at the time of initial purchase when interest, knowledge, and excitement are highest. Thus a marketer of computer-room furniture might, for market-selection and deployment purposes, segment its market into those customers who were recent purchasers of new computers and those who were not.

In some cases, companies that use particular products and services may be oriented to the use of similar, but not physically related, products or services. Some purchasers of plant equipment, for example, seem always to want the latest, most-efficient technology. Thus the purchaser of one advanced technology may also be a likely purchaser of another new, yet not related, technology. Such an interest or proclivity may be driven by other, more-fundamental variables, such as risk acceptance, technical sophistication, and so forth, but the vendor may find it harder to learn about these more-fundamental variables than, for example, to purchase a list of recent purchasers of a new device or service.

There are clear limits to the complementary-products approach. We have seen companies go to inordinate lengths to identify the cross-product usage patterns of their current customers without giving due consideration to the differences between current and prospective customers. While it is much easier to gather data on current customers because salespeople often have a great deal of access to information and companies at least know what they themselves have shipped to the customer, there is little to be gained from blindly extrapolating patterns of current buyers to prospects.

Despite our concerns about the blind acceptance of the complementary-products approach, we believe that it offers the opportunity for useful practitioner application and academic investigation.

Customer Capabilities

It makes good sense in performing segmentation for either market selection or program development to list the vendor's strengths on one side of a piece of paper and customers' operating weaknesses on the other. For market selection, the purpose is to look for dovetailing between what the customers need and what the vendor can supply. For program development, the purpose is to identify specific needs of market segments that the marketer can satisfy with tailored programs.

A zinc company captured a large share of the available market for zinc in the 1970s by judiciously matching its abilities to provide technical help and research aid to customers' needs. Although it, like all other vendors of this commodity, sold zinc in tonnage to steel mills and auto manufacturers, the firm concentrated its limited marketing dollars not in either of these segments but in marketing to the many small hot-dip galvanizing shops around the country. These smaller firms usually needed advice and laboratory help with their production problems and were receptive to selling their customers on the benefits of galvanizing using data provided by this zinc company.

There are many possibilities for segmenting a market based on financial competence, manufacturing competence, and technical competence. Operating executives use these variables, but academics have not yet considered them. Credit policy in the industrial-commercial sphere, for example, is an important variable to marketing and financial executives, and perhaps academics might find it useful as a research variable.

Assessment

Researchers who want to improve industrial-marketing practice could have a substantial impact if they study segmentation using either the user-nonuser dimension or customer capabilities. Both variables are used by practitioners, at least implicitly. The existing literature is sorely deficient on the operating-variables nest; however, a wealth of information can be compiled on prospects' and customers' operations, data that are slightly less easy to acquire than are demographic data. This information should comment on the prospect's technology-in-use, user-nonuser status, and technical, financial, and production capabilities.

5 The Middle Nest: Purchasing Approaches

The purchasing-approaches nest concerns the organization and dynamics of the buying center or decision-making unit (DMU) in the prospect organization, both internal to the company and in interaction with vendor firms. The literature on these variables is exceedingly rich and lends itself to the nested approach.

Collection of data about purchasing approaches requires at least some direct customer contact. Without such contact, it is almost impossible to get adequate information on the prospect's or customer's purchasing organization and processes, power structure, existing vendor-customer relationships of an institutional more than a personal nature, general purchasing policies, and criteria. To the extent that this information is available, the purchasing-approaches nest is more appropriate for companies with which the vendor has had some contact and about which the manager desires greater understanding for marketing and selling effectiveness. There is a great deal of information that can be put to use by the marketer interested in investigating the purchasing-approaches nest with prospects or customers.

Purchasing Organization

In his study of six major corporations' procurement strategies Corey (1978a) has identified procurement organization as a central variable for understanding how companies buy. He identified three general factors relating to purchasing organization and to the degree of purchasing function specialization: the different skills necessary to buy different types of products, the nature of the supply industry and ongoing supplier relationships, and the nature of internal purchasing relationships.

The major differentiating characteristic of purchasing organizations Corey identified was the degree of centralization of the purchasing function. He found that a number of variables seemed to

41

affect the degree of centralization. For one, commonality of requirements among diverse operation sites fosters centralization; diversity, on the other hand, fosters decentralization. "If standardization across a whole category of purchases is difficult, then a central buying group may well settle for picking off the high-volume items" (p. 96). Second, cost-saving potential can drive buyers toward centralization. This factor is partially dependent on the nature of the supply environment. If there are not any big industry suppliers that can serve a large user's needs, then the cost-savings potential of a centralized procurement function may be minimized.

Third, to the extent to which a single, centralized purchasing staff is able to "get down the experience curve" by developing specialized buying resources and not duplicating functions across the company's operating divisions, centralization is encouraged. Fourth, Corey found that the extent of engineering involvement in procurement decision making is an important determinant of whether purchasing centralization takes place. When engineering is deeply and regularly involved in the purchasing process, such as early in the product's development cycle or when the end product changes regularly, it is better for purchasing to be in close proximity to engineering. Decentralization is the result.

Fifth, the ordering and usage patterns of purchased items was found to have a major influence on the degree of purchasing centralization possible. When, for instance, a wide range of standard supply items is needed continually in small volumes, it makes more sense to decentralize buying tasks. When volume leverage is possible on such items, centralization is the preferred operating pattern. Finally, Corey found that the nature of the firm's relationships with its customers sometimes has a bearing on the location of the purchasing function. Large customers that issue multimillion dollar contracts, such as the federal government, may want a direct relationship with one purchasing manager assigned to the specific plant where the contract is being executed. Corey noted that the supply shortages of the mid-1970s provoked some companies to respond to this centralization of supply-side power with a centralization of their own buying power.

The message from Corey's research is clear and useful: it is possible to discover generalizations about purchasing organizations that are applicable for segmentation purposes. Centralization is one such variable. Across the six companies that Corey studied, several observable factors about the company and its purchasing situation seemed to suggest whether a centralized or decentralized structure would appear. In turn, the presence of a primarily centralized or decentralized purchasing structure has implications for potential vendors.

Generally large, national suppliers that can both work with a sophisticated central purchasing function and supply many operating sites are favored by the customer's centralization. On the other hand, smaller regional suppliers that cannot supply many disparate operating units or are relatively unsophisticated in their sales and account-management approaches often have problems serving a centralized purchaser. Thus centralization of the purchasing function is a relevant variable for market selection.

Because the centralized procurement function has different needs from the decentralized one, it also often requires different marketing and sales strategies, plans, and programs. A company with centralized purchasing is, for example, an appropriate subject for a national-account management approach. The decentralized customer, on the other hand, often does not desire or need such an approach. Centralized purchasers often stress price rather than local responsiveness and service, or they may demand custom products or services. These elements of the marketing approach can be tailored to the centralized and decentralized segments.

Power Structure

The Buying Center

In most important purchases, a number of managers and functional areas are involved, only some of which may have any formal purchasing responsibility.[1] In some cases, the managers who decide to buy a product never work through the purchasing function except to request issuance of a purchase order. The problem for the seller is to be aware of who will be in the buying decision-making group or buying center, how the group will interact, and who the influential people are who can make or break the decision. A further problem is to decide what impact this information should have on segmentation and segmented marketing programs.

One aspect of purchasing that remains constant regardless of the nature of the purchase or the buyers is the set of social tasks, or roles, that must be taken on for orderly purchase action to occur. This set of roles can be thought of as a more or less fixed set of behavioral pigeon holes into which different managers from different functional areas of the firm can be placed for different purchasing occasions. A complete set of roles specified for a single purchase is called a *buying center.* This concept of the buying center was proposed in its present form by Webster and Wind (1972).

Figure 5–1 shows six buying roles encountered in every purchasing situation. These roles are illustrated in the lower portion of the figure for the purchase or upgrade of a telecommunications system.

The initiator of the purchase process, whether for a corporate jet, paper towels, or communication services, is the individual (or individuals) who recognizes that a company problem can be solved or avoided by acquiring a product or service. In the communications example, the impetus may well be new technology or the lure of potential cost reductions through owning instead of leasing switching devices.

One or more gatekeeper(s) participate in the purchase process. They often are functional, problem, or product experts (perhaps purchasing managers) who are paid to be aware of the range of vendor offerings that may be employed to solve certain problems. In the telecommunications illustration, corporate purchasing, the corporate telecommunications staff, or, increasingly, data-processing experts may be involved. Through controlling information on products and vendor offerings, gatekeepers largely determine which vendors get in to sell and sometimes which vendors have access to corporate decision makers. For example, for some purchases the gatekeeping process is formalized through the use of an approved vendor list, which constitutes a written statement of who can sell to the firm.

Influencers are those managers who have some voice in whether a purchase is made and what is bought. The range of influencers becomes increasingly broad as purchases grow larger and the impact of the purchase broadens, as in data-processing equipment. In extreme cases, members of the board of directors can become influencers prior to a major decision.

The decider or deciders are those who make the decision on the contemplated purchase. Often with major purchases, some or all of the firm's senior management will carry out the decider role. Ordinarily, however, one of the involved individuals will assume a subrole of champion, or advocate, of the contemplated purchase and push it to completion. Without a champion or manager who acts as

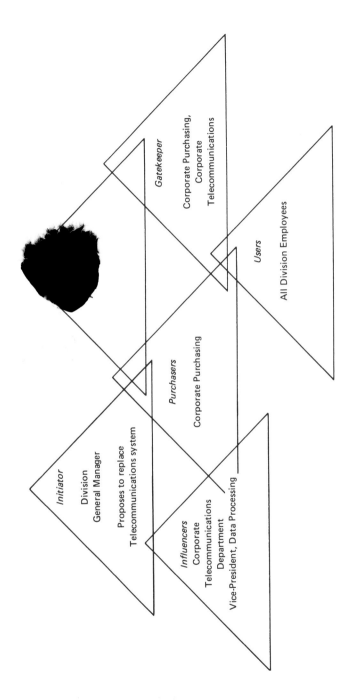

Figure 5-1. Buying Center

Source: Adapted from T.V. Bonoma, "Major Sales: Who *Really* Does the Buying?" *Harvard Business Review* 61 (May–June 1982):114.

an internal salesperson for the vendor's product, many purchases will never be made. It is important here to note that deciders often are not the individuals who authorize a purchase.

The roles of purchaser and user are those, respectively, concerned with obtaining and consuming the product or service in question. Corporate purchasing, often with financial and legal consultation, usually fills the first role. The second is filled variously depending on the product or service purchased.

This discussion pertains to social roles, not individuals or groups of individuals. In trivial purchase situations, such as a manager's buying a hand calculator on a business trip, one person will fill all six roles. The triangles in figure 5–1 collapse onto each other, such that the manager initiates (perceives a need for calculating power), gatekeeps ("What brand did I forget at home?"), in███████imself or herself ("This is more than I need, but it's only █████████ecides, purchases, and uses the equipment.

In major or complex buying situations, the n██████managers filling the basic roles will tend to be greater, altho███ the number will vary. Wesley J. Johnston and one of the authors, for example, studied sixty-two capital-equipment and service acquisitions in thirty-one firms (Johnston and Bonoma 1981). The decisions studied varied from plant-refuse disposal to plant expansion. For a typical capital-equipment purchase, an average of four departments (engineering and purchasing were always included), three levels of management (manager, regional manager, vice-president), and seven different individuals were involved in fulfilling the six buying roles. For services, the corresponding numbers were four departments, two levels of management, and five managers.

Another approach to understanding the number of people involved in a purchasing decision and their importance is the work done on the buying grid, or BUYGRID (Robinson, Faris, and Wind 1967). These authors hypothesized that there is a set number of stages through which all purchases can progress, though not every purchase goes through every stage. Figure 5–2 shows these stages across the columns, starting with the awareness of a problem needing solution and ending with an evaluation of the purchase made to solve that problem.

Robinson and colleagues claim that the critical factor in how the buying influentials in a firm approach any given purchase situation is their familiarity with the buying problem. In other words, purchasing

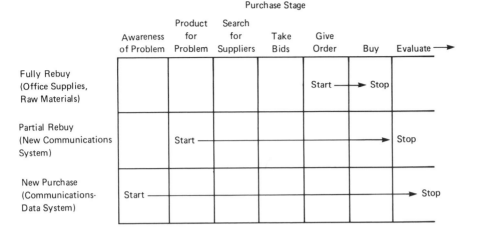

Figure 5-2. Buying Center by Stage: BUYGRID

Source: P.J. Robinson, C.W. Faris, and Y. Wind, *Industrial Buying and Creating Marketing* (Boston: Allyn and Bacon, 1967), p. 131. Reprinted with permission.

Note: The stages involved in the purchase expand as problem familiarity decreases and solution cost increases. The number of individuals involved in the buying center increases as problem familiarity decreases.

processes will differ depending upon how confident buyers are that the contemplated purchase could solve some problem. For some purchases, called *full rebuys,* buying is only a matter of reordering some regularly used product or service. There is near certainty that the product or service will apply as needed. In a second class of purchases, called *partial rebuys,* the buying influentials are dissatisfied with some aspect of the current performance of a product or service and wish to make their next purchase in a slightly different fashion so that perceived deficiencies can be removed or added functions achieved. Finally, in the *new-purchase* class are all those products or services with which the firm has had no prior experience and therefore no confidence that the purchase will provide the needed solution.

The major findings of the research done by Robinson and his colleagues on this type of matrix are that two phenomena occur. First, the stages of purchase depicted across the top of figure 5-2 are not equally implemented across all three product classes. The buying center will go through the fewest number of stages in the full rebuy situation. Usually a purchasing-department member will simply re-order the needed product or service from an existing supplier. More stages are enacted in the partial-rebuy situation, where at least an informal search for a new or modified product will be undertaken, bids invited, and some evaluation pursued. In the new-purchase situation, the buying center enacts all stages of the BUYGRID, usually including a lengthy postpurchase evaluation.

Second, Robinson and his colleagues found that the closer the situation is toward the new-purchase end of the continuum, the more likely it is that a larger number of individuals will become involved in the purchase. Conversely, the closer the product or service being looked at is to a full rebuy, the more likely it is that a smaller number of individuals (perhaps even one) will comprise the buying team.

Thus the buying process changes radically across the three applications-confidence categories identified by Robinson and colleagues. Some later research by Grønhaug (1975) confirms these findings in a cross-cultural context. Grønhaug found that more people became involved in specialty-store buying in Norway when the buying problem was more novel and when the goods were more likely to be resold than when the goods were being used as supplies.

There are certainly many other ways to think about the stages of the purchase process. One is to consider the process by which sources for purchases are arrived at. For many industrial goods the sourcing process often involves four stages, which are repeated on an annual basis or at some other predetermined frequency. The first stage is vendor qualification, which leads to a list of technically and formally qualified vendors. Criteria at this stage usually include product quality and vendor financial continuity. The long list is then cut to a short list of preferred vendors, each of which will receive some business. In the third stage, each vendor on the short list is allocated a theoretical share of the business. In many situations, the long list will include ten or more sources and the short list only three or four. A typical split of the business among three vendors might be 60 percent, 30 percent, and 10 percent. The fourth stage of the process is the actual release of orders on a day-to-day basis. At this point, the variance between the theoretical share allocated in phase 3 and the actual share allocated in the day-to-day release can be substantial, perhaps 5 to 10 percent of the total business.

The criteria applied at each stage differ. Long-list criteria tend to be measurable and formalistic with an emphasis on staying power and technical product quality. The short-list criteria might be price, service, and sales quality, and these same three criteria weighted differently might determine share allocation. The actual order release might depend upon the vendor's sales-call frequency and quality, very recent delivery reliability, and ability to ship quickly.

It would seem useful for a vendor to consider the criteria used at each stage and the stage at which the customer is in the sourcing process for segmentation purposes. Among the likely purposes here are analysis, sales forecasting, and sales-price development.

Much research has been done on the nature and operation of the buying center. Perhaps the first article to indicate that a number of people other than purchasing personnel are involved in buying decisions was that of Cyert, Simon, and Trow (1956). Their research found that programmed or routine decisions involved fewer firm members from different departments compared to unprogrammed or nonroutine decisions. Buzzell et al.'s (1972) marketing text contains a case noting the participation of twelve people in the routine purchase of a $3,000 air compressor. Brand (1972) conducted a study in the United Kingdom among companies employing over 250 persons. He found that general-management and technical personnel were perceived as equal in importance to or more important than the purchasing executives themselves in most purchasing decision phases. Patchen (1974) studied thirty-three different purchase situations in eleven heavy-manufacturing and light-manufacting firms. He found nearly twenty different individuals involved in important and eight different individuals involved in trivial purchase decisions.

The way in which companies buy is directly related to the role that different parts of the organization play in the purchase process. We have used the term *power structure* to represent the whole complex of roles and relationships among the organizational elements of the buying company, including such elements as engineering, procurement, and manufacturing. Most analyses of power structure have looked at the role of the formal purchasing function. We believe that a key issue in understanding that role is the evolution of the purchasing function as an organizational entity.

The position of the industrial purchasing manager varies a great deal across companies (Hill, Alexander, and Cross 1975). What in some companies is the total responsibility for materials management in the firm was once the merely clerical task of exchanging money for goods and recording the transactions as they occurred. There is a continuum of purchasing evolution, and not every corporation has evolved to the sophisticated view of purchasing suggested, for example, by Corey's research among major corporations like General Motors.

Risley (1972) has identified four distinct phases in the evolution of the industrial-buying role—buying, purchasing, procurement, and materials management—which represent different philosophies about the task of obtaining the materials and machinery needed by the firm to accomplish its goals. According to Risley, buying was the very low-level clerical task of handling the paperwork in purchasing. The negotiation of deals, including major agreements about price and delivery, was normally entrusted only to the most-senior procurement officers in the largest corporations and to senior general managers in most other firms.

As purchasing specialists began to appear, planning and policy perspectives were added to the buying job in the purchasing phase of evolution. A departmental organization emerged led by the purchasing manager and staffed by buyers. The industrial-procurement phase, the third evolutionary step along the continuum, included all phases of the purchasing job but added acquisition strategies (such as make versus buy), more-sophisticated procedures for vendor evaluation, product testing, formal communications systems between procurement executives and user sites, search procedures for new vendors and materials, and the forecasting of purchasing needs and price trends.

Finally, Risley claims, the materials-management phase represents the most-advanced evolutionary stage. Functions such as inventory control and excess-material utilization, policy formulation for decisions such as forward buying and joint buying, and legal considerations as well as research and development participation, all become legitimate concerns of the purchasing executive.

Where any corporation (and its purchasing staff) falls along this continuum will be a function of a number of factors, including both corporate and purchasing variables. If customers or prospects could be assigned to various points along this purchasing ladder, selling strategies tailored to each segment might well prove to be more profitable than a general approach. One of the authors, for example, has found in proprietary research that in certain industries, purchasing of mechanical construction services can be categorized largely as the buying phase of Risley's evolutionary scheme. In this phase top management exerts a great deal of influence over vendor choice. Not recognizing this, contractors have sold to procurement, plant, and engineering staff personnel. Thus the primary sales effort may have been misdirected toward people with little power.

In general, studies suggest that the size and complexity of the buying center increase with the importance of the purchase, its novelty or degree of risk to the prospective buyer, and its nature (capital equipment or service). The material on purchasing evolution, as well as Corey's research on the centralization of procurement, shows that the role of the procurement function in total and the relative role of various parts (for example, headquarters versus plant level buyers) vary from company to company.

Bases of Power

The next step in the analysis of power structure is to consider the different forms of power that exist and how they are exerted in a buying situation. Power means the regular ability to change the behavior of others in the company (see Kotter 1979). Power, however, does not correlate perfectly with organizational rank. The printing-press operator, for example, may have the ability to veto the company's decision to buy a particular new press on a technical basis. Frequently in purchase deliberations, employees with not much formal power have the ability to stop the purchase or at least to make its completion difficult. Similarly, low-power individuals can also facilitate a particular purchase decision. The purchasing manager who does not specify a vendor in disfavor as a potential supplier or the secretary who screens out one vendor's salespeople because of a real or imagined slight can change the purchasing outcome radically. This means that sales and marketing efforts cannot be directed through a simple reading of the prospect's organizational charts. What is needed are some reliable signals for identifying the powerful buying-center members.

Over twenty years ago psychologists J.R.P. French, Jr., and Bertram Raven (1959) offered a scheme of five power bases, which has been subjected to a great deal of testing and modification. Figure 5-3 outlines these bases. In addition the figure shows our categorization of the powerful buying-center members' influence into that which is positive, or champion, power and that which is primarily

Type of Power	Direction	Definition Champion	Veto
Reward power	Ability to provide monetary, social, political, or psychological rewards to others for compliance	X	
Coercive power	Ability to provide monetary or other punishments for noncompliance	X	
Attraction power	Ability to elicit compliance from others because they like you	X	X
Expert power	Ability to elicit compliance because of technical expertise, either actual or reputed		X
Status power	Compliance-gaining ability deriving from a legitimate position in a company		X

Source: Adapted from T.V. Bonoma, "Major Sales: Who *Really* Does the Buying?" *Harvard Business Review* 61 (May–June 1982):114.

Figure 5–3. Bases of Power

negative, or veto, power. Champion power is the ability to specify a vendor, veto power the ability to exclude a vendor.

The first two power bases in figure 5–3 are reward and coercive power. Reward power refers to a manager's ability to provide others with monetary, social, political, or psychological benefits. Coercive power, on the other hand, refers to a manager's ability to impose punishments on others. It is important to note two things about the use of reward and coercive power in the organization. The first is that individuals who threaten punishment or promise reward do not necessarily actually have coercive power or reward power. Those managers who are most vocal are sometimes the least able to deliver on their words. The second point is that those who can reward and punish others in the organization may or may not be the individuals holding the highest formal management rank. In fact, research suggests that peers, not superiors, are the major source of reward and punishment power in most organizations (see Bonoma and Zaltman 1981).

The third power base, attraction power, refers to a manager's ability to get others to go along with his or her preferences because of liking. Next to the ability to reward and punish, attraction is the most-potent power base in managerial life. Often the power of being liked can be used by a manager to get his or her way in buying situations where cruder forms of influence would fail.

When a manager gets others to go along with his or her judgment because of real or perceived expertise in some area, expert power is being invoked. The skills attributed to the expert need not be real, if by real we mean that the individual actually possesses skills not held by others. It is enough that others believe the expert has special skills or are willing to respect his or her opinion on a topic because of expertise in a totally unrelated area. Expertise is a broad and generalizable power base in the corporation since it rests on reputed rather than actual skills.

Finally, there is status power, or the power that comes from having a high position in the corporation. This notion of power is most akin to what is meant by the word *authority*. It refers to the kind of influence a president has over a first-line supervisor and is both more restricted and more forceful than most of the other power bases.

Corporations, buying centers, and individual managers generally display one dominant power base. It may be customary in a firm's culture to influence others primarily on expertise, status, or some other typical power base, although the tactics of individual managers may vary. In one small company, for example, appeal is almost constantly (and dysfunctionally) made to whether the manager arguing a position is a family member (related to the founders of the firm and therefore having the status authority that comes from history and financial investment).

The last two columns of figure 5–3 show that the type of power invoked may allow the manager to exert champion or veto influence, but not always both. Generally we believe that holders of status and expert power tend to employ their power to veto decisions with which they do not agree. Holders of reward and coercive power more often push through purchases and the choice of favored vendors. Attraction power is used to champion and veto. Nevertheless, the central point here is that for many buying-center members, power tends to be unidirectional. Corporate financial officers, for example, are often cited as prime examples of managers' holding strong veto power in corporations where margins are thin or growth is poor.

It is not always easy to assess the power of each individual in the buying center. The literature strongly suggests that the vendor cannot rely solely on prospect managers' (especially the purchasing function's) perception of who is important to the buying process. Weigand (1966), for example, has reported findings from a study to determine the perceived responsibilities of a group of purchasing agents. He compared their responses to the opinions of other executives in the same firm and found that purchasing managers rated themselves as more central and more important to the purchasing process than other executives perceived them to be. Similarly purchasing managers tended to perceive themselves as having great concern for product design, application costs, choice of manufacturer, engineering help, and other variables far more often than did other executives who rated the purchasing managers. This general pattern of findings has also been reported by de Rijcke (1978).

Cooley, Jackson, and Ostrom (1977) asked managers from various functional areas in a firm to judge who had power over different buying phases. They found that perceptions of purchasing's power differed significantly when supplier selection was the issue as opposed to when product selection itself was at stake. The purchasing department's power was rated high in the first case and low in the second case.

Strauss (1962), in a classic article, conducted field interviews and administered questionnaires to 142 purchasing agents. He found that their work behavior was strongly influenced by lateral relationships—that is, informal influence from their peers in the buying center—rather than by their superiors or subordinates. Strauss found that the skillful purchasing managers used a variety of techniques to get their way in the legitimized conflict of the buying center, including invoking corporate rules when that was consistent with their aims, and recommending that policies be circumvented when that suited their ends.

The implication that emerges for segmentation analysis from this research is clear: purchasing managers feel they are more central to the buying process than other managers in the firm will substantiate. Purchasing managers interact mainly with their peers, who fill many of the remaining roles in the buying center and are only one part of a complex buying reality even in the most-progressive corporations (see Corey 1978).

The seller must determine from observation, not just opinion, the composition of the buying center; however, the problem of identifying the powerful buying-center members still remains. Figure 5–4 lists six clues to identifying the powerful individuals. We have distilled these clues from empirical research, most of it from psychology, and have found that these behavioral signs are more efficient than examination of formal organizational charts or use of informal power signs such as office size.

Clue 1 says that although power and formal authority do not inevitably go together, there is often a correlation between the two. Thus it just restates the cliché that the more-powerful buying-group members, or the influencers and decision makers in our role terms, are more likely to have higher management positions.

Our second generalization suggests that one way to identify powerful buying-center members is to observe the communications that occur in the buying company. Behavioral research confirms that the powerful are not threatened by others, nor are they promised rewards very often. Rather, the less powerful influence the more powerful through persuasion, expertise, and attraction. Ingratiation, or falsely claiming attraction toward the superior and touting his or her accomplishments, is a particularly strong subset of attraction power used to influence decision makers. Other kinds of influence

Clue 1:   Power and authority (corporate rank) are not the same but are often correlated.

Clue 2:   Powerful buying influencers and decision makers are influenced primarily by expertise or attraction, not by reward or punishment.

Clue 3:   Decision makers are often disliked moderately and viewed as strong but as somewhat bad by the less powerful.

Clue 4:   Decision makers tend to be one-way information centers for their group. They may or may not share what they know, but others usually share with them.

Clue 5:   Influencers and decision makers are likely to be neither the most-visible nor the most-talkative members of buying groups.

Clue 6:   There is no invariant relationship between functional area and power across firms.

Source: Adapted from T.V. Bonoma, "Major Sales: Who *Really* Does the Buying?" *Harvard Business Review* 61 (May–June 1982):115.

Figure 5-4. Clues to Identifying Influencers and Decision Makers in the Buying Center

used by the weaker on the stronger include rational argument and expertise, which can be used in an attempt to modify the power holder's position. Thus if there are one or several buying-center members to whom many others direct much persuasive attention but toward whom few rewarding or coercive actions seem directed, that individual may possess substantial decision-making power.

Interestingly, finding 3 suggests that buying-center decision makers may be disliked moderately by those not having as much power. Also, the less-powerful managers in such a relationships are likely to view the power holder as strong but evaluate him or her somewhat negatively as well. This duality can be put to good use by salespeople. Where there appears to be much concern on the part of others about one buying member's opinions but yet some expressed dislike of or ambivalence toward him or her, salespeople have almost certainly identified a critical buyer for sales attention.

Clue 4 argues that powerful buyers tend to be one-way information centers for their groups. This means that the decision maker is not a frequent provider of information to the group but rather serves as a focal point for information from others. For example, the vice-president who does not come to meetings but who seems to be the recipient of copies of all correspondence about buying matters is probably a central influencer or decider.

In a related vein, clue 5 suggests that the most-powerful buying-center members are likely to be neither the most-identifiable nor the most-talkative members of their groups. Indeed the really powerful buying-group member often sends others to critical negotiations because he or she is comfortable that little of substance will be concluded without his or her participation or approval.

Finally, observation 6 cautions that regardless of normal or usual relationships, there is no stable correlation across firms between the functional area of a manager and his or her power. It is not possible to approach the data-processing department on the unquestioned assumption that it will contain the decision makers for a new computer system, as many mainframe computer salespeople have learned. Nor can one simply look to the chief executive officer to find a decision maker for a corporate plane. There is no substitute for hard work and knowing the company and its buying dynamics. With close observation, the seller can identify the buying-center members and cull the powerful using those techniques.

Power and Segmentation

The key conclusions of the literature on power structure are these:

1. The roles that must be filled in any buying center are fairly constant.
2. Many people are often involved in a decision purchase.
3. The size and complexity of the buying center increase with the importance of the purchase, its risk or novelty, and its nature (capital equipment or service).
4. The role of the purchasing function varies across companies and across time for individual companies.
5. The role of various parts of the purchasing function varies.
6. There are different kinds of power.
7. It is important to identify the holders of power and the amount and kind of power they hold.
8. It is possible though difficult to identify the power holders and to assess the amount and kind of power they hold.

These conclusions hold many implications for market-segmentation purposes such as market selection, the development of sales strategies, and the choice of the role that each element of the marketing mix will play in a segmented-marketing program. For example, some companies will find it impossible to sell to a large and complex buying center, while others with a strong account orientation will find such situations particularly appropriate for their distinctive competitive skills. Also, because the size and complexity of the buying center varies over time in a given company, it would appear that market-segmentation schemes and the plans and programs built around them will also have to vary.

Identifying power holders is particularly important for segmentation purposes. To illustrate, generally the purchasing organization is very price sensitive. Thus in situations where the purchasing organization is powerful, price may play a more-important role than in other companies where the purchasing function is less powerful. A seller might use this knowledge to select customers appropriate to its strengths or perhaps to develop programs such as setting up a separate price-oriented operating unit to appeal to price-oriented buyers. On the other hand, delivery service is important to procurement people. Therefore a company may develop special delivery programs for customers with strong procurement functions or may choose to emphasize or deemphasize such customers and prospects depending upon its ability to deliver on time. Advertising and promotional programs, and even the sales force, can also be tailored to meet the special interests of the powerful members of the buying center.

Chapter 2 mentioned the potential application of segmentation at strategic levels as well as tactical levels and drew distinctions between the needs of, for example, salespeople and strategic planners. Power structure is an excellent variable for exemplifying these distinctions and, at the same time, identifying shared interests.

To achieve tactical goals, sales programs can be customized at the individual buying-influence level to appeal to certain kinds of power. Discounts or offers of price reductions may not be especially meaningful to a manager in the senior selling company who is most concerned with status power, while a visit by senior selling-company management may prove effective in flattering the ego and making the sale. Similarly sales management may wish to provide expert selling appeals to engineers or other buying-company staff who generally base their power on expertise. A salesperson might use the power-structure variable to decide which prospect to devote a great deal of time to and which prospect to write off.

Strategic-level choices can be made on similar bases. In fact, in some cases they must be. If one were designing a product for which there were many price-features trade-offs, one would have to forecast the demand for products that were feature rich and those that were low in cost. One useful way to do so would be to separate the market into price-sensitive and feature-sensitive segments, a difficult task. However, one might approach the task by attempting, based on sales force and other data, to divide buyers into engineering-dominated and purchasing-dominated groups. Implementation might not be easy, but the conceptual approach and the application of the approach are clear.

One hypothesis that may arise from the conscious or unconscious implementation of such selective marketing programs is that companies will best serve customers with similar power structures. That is, technically oriented vendors will eventually gravitate to selling primarily to technically oriented customers. This hypothesis requires more research.

In sum, we believe that there are many segmentation approaches using the power variable that are useful for analysis, market selection, and program development at several levels in the company.

Nature of Existing Relationship

Perhaps the most-important literature on buyer-seller relationships is that related to source loyalty. The concept of source loyalty, though difficult to define for research purposes (see Wind 1970), is nonetheless important for understanding industrial-buying behavior and segmentation. The reasons a buyer initially selects a particular vendor are not necessarily the same reasons it continues to purchase from this source. When the buyer comes into contact with the seller, evaluates the seller and available alternatives, makes the selection, and evaluates the results, it has established the framework for future relationships. Should both parties have a high enough level of satisfaction with the results, loyalty can become established. If the requirement for purchasing recurs, the strength of the satisfactory interaction may encourage the buyer to remain loyal. The buyer-seller relationship is dynamic, however, and subject to external changes, as well as changes within the dyad.

Arndt (1979) has recently written a provocative theoretical article in which he contends that long-term buyer-seller relationships are on the rise and fast becoming a customary market-interaction pattern, especially in the industrial arena. He argues that the tools needed to study such long-term relationships and, more important, the skills needed to compete in an arena where many potential customers are locked in to their current suppliers, are radically different from those needed in a less-stable marketing system. There is a great need for further research into the causes and consequences of such stable marketing relationships.

Despite the possible trends toward stable market relationships, it may be possible to make good guesses as to when competitors' accounts are most approachable. Although it is difficult for vendors to identify individual firms that are likely to be dissatisfied with their current supplier, recent price increases, delivery problems, specification failures, component delays, and a host of other factors may reflect general or company-specific factors that the potential selling firm (with good intelligence and timing) can use to its advantage.

Luffman (1975) examined the manner in which the buyer searches the market for vendors. Receptivity to new vendors, according to Luffman, was highest during turbulent buying times, such as when dissatisfaction existed with a current supplier or when a new component was introduced. The actual extent of buyer search for a new vendor, however, was low. Senior management from outside the purchasing department were often involved in the decision to discontinue business with a current supplier, but the activity of searching for a new supplier was the responsibility of the purchasing function.

Source selection and loyalty characteristics can be used together for segmentation purposes. For instance, a firm could differentiate its customers by loyal and nonloyal groups. A typology consisting of various product lines or market conditions (shortage, normal, oversupply) might be laid over these two groups to help determine if they react differently in different situations. If loyal customers are more likely to switch in times of oversupply, for example, and nonloyal customers more likely to switch in times of shortage, it may be possible to develop differentiated marketing programs to achieve the desired results. Additionally it might be possible to review prospects to identify those who are likely to switch. Some of these concepts could just as easily be called situational variables as purchasing variables (see chapter 6).

The individuals in the buying center interact in complex ways. Some may have relationships with one vendor, while others may have relationships with another vendor. Such relationships may take many forms, including past purchase experience while employed by another company or even past employment at the vendor. The same is true of vendor personnel. The interaction of prospect (or customer) personnel with each other, and the interaction of these people with vendor personnel, will help to determine the outcome of the purchase process.

It is important to attempt to work simultaneously with the concepts of personal relationships, power structure, and organizational relationships. Good integration among these concepts will significantly improve the predictive and segmentation capabilities of the analytical process. A useful by-product of this analytical process is that it improves the ability of sales personnel to understand complex buying processes and gives them the insight about their specific accounts and the people in their accounts that they need to be most effective. The result is a situation where better segmentation also leads to better field execution of marketing plans and programs.

General Purchasing Practices and Policies

In contrast to some of the other purchasing variables, such as power structure, there is almost no literature on general purchasing policies. This section expands briefly on the concept and provides some examples that we believe can be generalized to many situations.

General purchasing policies may be explicit or implicit. The explicit policies are often the result of a careful review of business and economic factors. This review process may be complex and can involve as many people as the most major purchase decision a company makes. A policy of lease versus buy often is the subject of a careful review that considers the cost and availability of capital versus the cost and availability of lease financing. (We are referring to a financially oriented lease, not one that is actually a trial offer by the vendor.) Firm policies related to procurement from minority-owned vendors or small vendors are also typical examples of explicit policies.

Some general purchasing policies, on the other hand, are implicit and are the result of cultural biases within the company or of habit and tradition. For example, a company with a conservative culture that punishes mistakes with fervor but does not reward innovation well will probably end up with procurement policies favoring well-known, familiar vendors and preclude the selection of new vendors even if their products, services, and approaches are innovative and appropriate to the company's needs.

The implicit policies are much more difficult to identify than the explicit ones but are no less important. In fact, their influence may be more pervasive because they are strongly tied to culture and tradition. In addition, they are much harder to change than explicit policies. The latter are identifiable and usually concern matters that can be discussed in a rigorous, clear process. The former often concern subjects considered inappropriate for overt or formal discussion. Changing them often requires changing the company's culture and reward system and the personal biases of company personnel, a long process at best.

A good example of a mix of explicit and implicit general purchasing policies is a company's approach to the purchase of systems versus components. A company policy of purchasing total systems instead of procuring the pieces of the system independently might reflect very lean or weak engineering and purchasing operations. It might also reflect a company's conservative approach or fear that in buying the parts of a system separately it will end up with incompatible pieces or arguments among the piece vendors about relative responsibility for performance of the total system. The system-versus-components policy might be manifest in a wide variety of individual purchasing situations, such as for computer and telecommunications systems. It may also be manifest in less-obvious situations. The company might prefer to buy a new building in finished form from a developer rather than to purchase the land and hire an architect and a general contractor to build one. It certainly would not play the role of a general contractor itself and purchase the services of subcontractors. We might surmise that the same company would buy transportation services from a shipping-line company that develops packages of services, including truck, rail, and ocean shipping. The company would be a good prospect for an air-freight forwarder but a poor one for an airline that provided only the air shipment but not the ground connections.

As this example shows, general purchasing policies can be pervasive in a company. The marketer can treat such policies as a segmentation variable for market selection or for tailoring marketing programs to individual segments. In the example, a transportation company might offer packaged services to the systems segment and unbundled services to the components segment.

The centralization-decentralization issue has a great impact on general purchasing policies and thus on segmentation. A supplier of a small-package delivery service might need one communications program for companies that purchase all such services through a central mail or supply room and another communications program for companies in which each individual executive or secretary purchases the service.

Purchasing Criteria

Different companies seem to use different criteria in making their purchasing decisions. Criteria result from purchasing policies and power structure, but they are important enough to warrant separate discussion. This section looks first at the literature on criteria and then at that on the measurement system for procurement personnel, which we believe has a major impact on criteria. For this section we acknowledge a debt to Wesley Johnston's (1979) review.

Banville and Dornoff (1973) found that neither economic theory nor pure behavioral theory correctly represented the industrial source-selection process. In the group of builders of single-family homes whom they studied, service was the most-influential motive in source selection. Quality of the product ranked second, followed by supplier reputation, low price, geographical proximity, friendship with the salesperson, salesperson's personality, credit, prestige, reciprocity, and improvement of buyer's status within the firm. The ranking of these criteria changed somewhat with firm size and particular product class.

In a study on industrial source-selection variables, Perreault and Russ (1976) explored the effect of characteristics of physical-distribution service on purchase decisions. The survey found that physical-distribution service ranked second only to product quality in influencing industrial-purchase decisions. This finding possibly may be attributed to the scarcity of raw materials and the shortage economy of the mid-1970s. Some of the most frequently cited elements of physical-distribution service were order-cycle time, delivery-time variability, rush service, and order-status information. These findings have some benefit-segmentation implications, one of which is that rather than concentrating on simply minimizing the total cost of the distribution system, the marketing manager can look for differences between customers and potential customers in the benefits sought from distribution.

Some purchase criteria of high potential utility for segmentation stem directly from the measurement system used by customers for their procurement personnel. Case evidence would support the clear utility of using information on measurement systems for purchase personnel in segmentation. In one case, a small computer producer found it was getting an unusually high proportion of single-unit sales and having difficulty selling to its large national accounts. This vendor had adopted the seemingly sensible and conservative practice of listing lower book prices for its equipment; it then allowed correspondingly lower discounts during selling negotiations. In the large-customer segment, however, companies informally measured purchasing managers not by the total cost of the systems they bought but by the size of the discount negotiated for volume purchases. The vendor experienced significant buyer resistance because its discounting policy ran counter to the purchase criteria used by these large buyers.

Clearly the same approach can be used for all people involved in the purchasing process. In his study of procurement in six corporations, Corey (1978) pointed to the influence of internal purchasing measurement systems, as well as measuring systems of other functional areas on purchasing behavior. Corey found that the following areas of performance regularly concerned purchase supervisors:

1. facilitating the mission of those who use products by getting on-time deliveries of appropriate quality;
2. negotiating acceptable prices;
3. conforming to purchasing-function norms and expectations, such as maintaining good relations with suppliers or locating minority vendors; and
4. managing resources pertinent to sourcing and controlling purchasing-overhead expenditures.

There is a need for both academics and businesspeople to link results like Corey's with the purchasing criteria they lead to and the impact they can thus have on segmentation.

Purchase criteria are easy to relate to market selection and the development of segmented marketing programs. Clearly the marketer wants to choose customers whose purchase criteria it can meet. A vendor with a major brand name should emphasize customers and prospects who favor such a criterion. The purchase-criteria variables, in conjunction with the application variables, discussed in the next chapter, are particularly useful for the process of benefit segmentation.

Purchasing criteria often are a result of the power structure and the general purchasing policies. Thus there may be some overlap if both criteria and either power structure or general purchasing policies are used as segmentation dimensions. In some cases the redundancy will add a richness and insight to the process; in others it will add nothing but effort and cost.

An Integrated View

The purchasing-approaches nest of our segmentation scheme is very useful, and the literature on it is generally rich. Although much more research could be cited here, the general picture that emerges about the internal and external influences on buying is consistent with Walsh's (1961, p. 170) early judgment: "the chain of influences in most industrial buying situations is long, involved, and even mysterious." One reason for the mystery noted by Walsh is the subtle interaction among the parts of the purchasing-approaches nest, such as that between criteria and general purchasing policies. Clearly much more detailed research must be undertaken by academics if a more-complete view is to be obtained. Such research could have immediate applicability for managers' segmentation purposes by tying together much of what is now known only piecemeal about the complex interplay of interpersonal behavior, power politics, and criteria. Two recent studies stand out as examples of this kind of integrated knowledge gathering.

Johnston (1979) concluded an important study on buying groups in thirty-one companies. One capital-equipment and one industrial-service purchase was studied in each firm. Johnston measured aspects of the purchase itself (purchase novelty, complexity, and importance) and organizational characteristics (corporate size, formalization, centralization of authority, and organizational complexity). He defined four central buying-center aspects based on a theory of industrial buying behavior: (1) how many levels of the organizational hierarchy exerted influence on the purchase, called *vertical involvement*; (2) how many different departments and divisions exerted influence on the purchase, or *lateral involvement*; (3) the total number of individuals involved in the purchasing process, called *differentiation*; and (4) how much the members of the decision making unit communicated among themselves during the purchasing process, called *integrative complexity*. Johnston found the following empirical relationships held over a wide variety of industrial manufacturers:

Communications in the buying center increased as the purchase became more important. Spoken communication increased at a much greater rate than did written communications, however, indicating the importance of word of mouth in the buying group.

Purchase importance, novelty, and complexity had important roles in determining buying-center interaction and buyer-seller interaction. For example, the more novel a purchase situation, the more likely pricing was to be negotiated rather than simply

set by the seller in the case of capital equipment or settled by
competitive bidding in the case of industrial services.

Moriarty (1980) focused on bridging the gap between the concepts of organizational buying behavior and the practice of industrial-
market segmentation. He gathered a variety of behavioral variables
from multiple decision-making unit numbers in companies that had
purchased nonintelligent data terminals. His results showed that
behavioral profiles of buyers were useful for two cases:

1. Developing marketing strategies for market segments, including a
    segment based on the brand currently being used by the com-
    pany. For example, in the data-terminal market, IBM buyers
    differ significantly from non-IBM buyers on the importance of
    certain product benefits, the use of formal and informal sources
    of information, brand loyalty, innovativeness, and size of the
    purchase.
2. Developing new market segments based on the benefits sought by
    industrial buyers. For example, Moriarty identified four segments
    of data-terminal buyers: hardware buyers who were price sen-
    sitive; brand buyers who were concerned about pleasing their top
    management by making a safe decision; people buyers who de-
    pended heavily on the competence of the sales representative and
    were concerned about the person-machine interface (with regard
    to data terminals); and one-stop buyers who wanted a fully aug-
    mented product and a broad product line from which to choose.

Moriarty suggested how these benefit segments might be identified
by selling firms using the traditional macrosegmentation variables of
industry sector and company size, as well as the microsegmentation
variables of organizational level and functional area. These aspects of
Moriarty's work are discussed in the next chapter.

The Johnston and Moriarty studies are valuable first steps in inte-
grating what is known about the purchasing-approaches nest for segmentation purposes. Much more of this sort of work must be done
before we have a reliable composite of buying-center operations.

6

The Inner-Middle Nest: Situational Factors

The situational variables and the personal variables change more frequently than variables in the previous nest. The decision to consider the situational-variables nest as exterior to the personal-characteristics nest is not clear-cut. One might make an argument that the personal-characteristics nests should be exterior to the situational-factors nest because situational factors are even more temporary than personal characteristics. The situational and personal nests could even have been placed at the same level.

The situational factors considered in this chapter are:

Application,

Type and size of purchase,

Environmental situation, and

Situational buying risk.

Little published work has been done in this area. Most of what has been done has focused on application.

Application

Often one product has several possible applications. If there are reliable patterns across customers and product lines of differences in use, then usage can serve as an especially profitable segmentation basis.

There have been two major works on application. The first is a 1970 study by *Scientific American,* which developed information on the differences in the purchase of raw materials, supplies, and components. The second is the study by Moriarty (1980).

The publishers of *Scientific American* provide some good evidence for the usefulness of looking at product applications in *How Industry Buys.* For their study, they questioned individuals in over six hundred firms about which functional areas became involved and the amount of influence each had in the purchase of three categories of goods: goods intended to be applied at the front end of the production process as raw materials, goods to be used as prefabricated components during assembly, and supplies used to support production. Two findings stand out. The first is that substantially different patterns regarding involvement and influence of buying-center members were evident for each of the three classes of application. Design engineering was dominant at many purchase stages for components purchases, while other parties (such as production engineering) were more important for raw-material purchases. Second, for all three kinds of purchases, there was a clear pattern of dominance by the engineering function at the initiating and determining-kind purchase stages and increasing importance of the purchasing function only in the decision-on-supplier stage (figure 6–1).

For the present purpose, what is important to recognize is that raw materials were purchased somewhat differently from components, and both of these were purchased differently from supplies. These findings are of relevance to companies making products that can be used as either supplies or components, such as fasteners and electrical components. They are also useful for companies selling products that can be used either as components or capital equipment, such as technical computers purchased by end users as capital equipment and by OEMs as components for their computer-controlled equipment or systems. Marketers will have to create different marketing programs for OEMs and end users because of the different purchase processes and the different benefits of interest.

One way to think about applications is to consider it as a link between the industry variable and the particular benefits desired by companies. A vendor may find that either industry, applications, or benefits alone or any combination of the three may be a useful way to segment the market. Moriarty's work (1980) demonstrated a possible way to use this approach for one product, nonintelligent computer terminals. Moriarty studied the purchase process for this equipment in 319 buying groups, spread across five different industries (business services, transportation, wholesale-retail trade, financial services, and manufacturing). On the basis of previous studies, each industry was believed to have a differing application for the terminals. For instance, retailers generally employed their terminals for customer-service applications, and manufacturers generally employed terminals for order-entry and inventory-control applications.

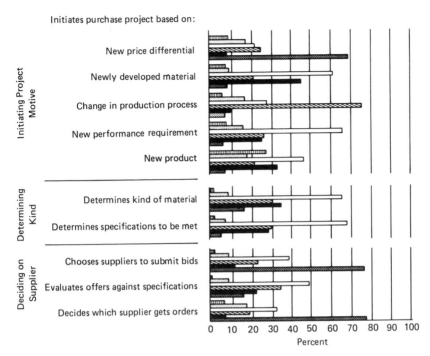

Initiates purchase project based on:

Note: Bars show the frequency of purchasing involvement at each step of the purchasing process for these six most-mentioned management functions:

Overall corporate policy and planning   Production engineering

Operations and administration   Research

Design and development engineering   Purchasing

Figure 6-1. How Industry Buys Materials

Moriarty asked each decision participant in the buying group to evaluate the importance of thirty-three selection criteria in picking a vendor. The criteria ranged from "offers a broad line of hardware" to "salesperson's competence." These criteria were reduced by statistical analysis to fourteen benefits, which were used to distinguish one group of decision participants from another. In order of importance across all decision participants, the top seven desired benefits were: (1) service; (2) reliability; (3) manufacturer's stability; (4) software; (5) compatibility with current and future systems; (6) delivery; and (7) speed.

Moriarty then split his respondents into benefit segments, or groups of respondents who wanted a similar set of benefits from a nonintelligent data terminal purchase. In one analysis, he found two major benefit segments in his data—one that preferred low prices and ease of operation and another that desired a broad hardware and software line and a stable and safe manufacturer. These benefit segments make sense; one group is probably experienced in terminal buys and wants good quality with low prices, while the other, probably less-experienced, group wants to minimize its risks and minimize the number of vendors with whom it works. When Moriarty drew a matrix of industry group versus benefit segment ("price" buyers or "brand" buyers), he found the pattern shown in figure 6-2.

By determining the benefits that different users want and relating these to industry, Moriarty supplies the industrial marketer of nonintelligent data terminals with three important pieces of knowledge about the market: what different benefit groups exist, how these groups are allocated across industries, and a specification of who to sell to and how to sell to them. For example, a nondominant terminal vendor probably would do better to concentrate on the wholesale-retail, finance, and manufacturing industries and to compete with low prices, no frills, but exceptionally competent salespeople. An industry leader, by contrast, should expect easier sales among risk-averse buyers, who will probably pay premium prices for breadth of product line and the believed safety of the brand. Although Moriarty looked at industries that were thought to be synonymous with

Group	Price Buyer	Brand Buyer
Business services		X
Wholesale-retail	X	
Finance	(slight tendency)	
Manufacturing	X	

Figure 6-2. Summary of Moriarty's Findings

specific applications, it would be possible to use a similar approach to look at one or more industries where there are multiple applications and to relate these to benefit groups.

As an example of applications segmentation, consider the four manufacturers that compete for the continuous-coal-mining-machine market in the United States. Users generally operate only one or two vendors' machines at most, since the spare-parts inventory and service requirements quickly get prohibitive as the number of brands increases. Two of the manufacturers make relatively standard, off-the-shelf miners. One manufactures semicustom machinery that has a moderately strong reputation for being able to work in hard-mining conditions (that is, where rock is encountered). The fourth competitor makes machines designed especially for hard mining. By watching the sales patterns of the other hard-rock machine, this last company was able to make sales presentations to coal companies that it believed had both a need and a desire for their specialized machine.

Type and Size of Purchase

Among purchase variables are the size of order, immediacy of need, and order mix. These variables are closely related to the customer's size and purchasing approach, including the degree of centralization of the procurement function, but they are not totally determined by them. As with many other variables, a supplier can choose to use these segmentation dimensions as a way to select (or select out of) specific market segments or as a way to develop tailored approaches to specific market segments. For instance, some suppliers choose to accommodate large orders or even individual line entries on an order, and others prefer small ones. Then volume discounts can be used to encourage or discourage large orders. The company's product policy, including delivery reliability, inventory-carrying capability, and excess-production capacity, might be varied for the different interests of each customer segment. However, the company should monitor such an approach carefully, for it can be expensive and not too profitable.

Consider the electrical wholesaler that stocks cable, wiring devices, and conduit as its primary inventory. This intermediary usually deals with two classes of customer. The first is large accounts—customers that buy only a few of the many items inventoried by the wholesaler but in large quantities and with regularity. The second group is the basket contractors—small businesses that generally buy a number of varied products in small quantities. The first segment is comfortable with long lead times; the second needs carry-out purchases, from stock. This is common knowledge in the industry. What is not, but is used for segmentation purposes by the most-astute and profitable wholesalers, is that some of the basket contractors act more like their larger counterparts, ordering in quantity and with some lead time. This business, because it does not receive the same discounts as the higher quantity orders of the major accounts, can be highly profitable to the wholesalers. Furthermore, some larger contractors act like their smaller counterparts because of inefficient materials planning. A major account might discover that someone in the organization forgot to order the special dimmer switches for a building and call a wholesaler with an emergency order. Having the ability to satisfy urgent needs more quickly than competitors can also be profitable.

The large contractors that experience emergencies over time tend to be the same ones. The small contractors that plan their usage better than the average basket contractor also tend to be the same companies. The wholesaler that studies sales records by account and by line item on the order can segment users by the nature of their order. In this case, the relevant dimensions are emergency versus lead time. By planning for the large users' emergencies and working to identify the good planners among small contractors, the wholesaler is in the position of giving high customer satisfaction and reaping high profits.

Environmental Situation

A number of environmental factors can lead to ways to segment markets. Among these are raw-material shortages, the regulatory climate, general inflation or interest rates, and industry structure. A creative way to view such situations is as segmentation over time, not across different types of companies or people.

Luffman (1975) found that receptivity to new vendors is highest during turbulent times such as the introduction of a new product. Environmental factors such as shortages can change the buying process. A company might use its resources to compete for customers during shortage periods when the customers are most sensitive to availability and most willing to add new suppliers. The hope would be that the new supplier would be maintained as a regular source in normal times. In such a situation, a company's prices might fluctuate greatly depending upon the supply-demand balance in the industry. Chemical traders seem to use that type of strategy with a clear understanding that profits will fluctuate as well.

Risk

Risk deserves special attention because it has a large impact on the purchase process and the way in which individuals behave. Here, risk is considered in terms of risk-reduction and risk-sharing processes at the group level. The next chapter looks at risk-reduction processes among individuals. At the group level, some of these processes are related to the nature of the people involved, their previous history, and their culture as a group. It is the situation, however, that generates the risk to which the people, individually and in groups, must respond. Let us look at the relationship between risk and the three situational variables already considered.

Application plays a great role in determining risk. Also the concept of risk is central to an understanding of the importance of application. If the operation of a refinery pump is necessary to the safety of the refinery, the pump motor will not be purchased in the same way as if the pump were not out of the ordinary. One reason that OEM customers demand a different marketing approach from end-user customers is that the component being supplied is often central to the total business of the OEM. This is not generally true with the end user. There is evidence that when purchases have a high risk of failure, some buyers tend to focus on brand familiarity (Moriarty 1980).

Environmental shortages and other forms of environmental turbulence increase risk and change its nature. During a shortage the risk of overpaying is generally much less than the risk of being without the product. Again, the impact of the environmental situation cannot be considered without careful consideration of risk.

Finally, type of purchase and order size affect risk. A large order, by its very nature, involves more dollars and greater risk associated with quality and delivery than does a small order. Urgency of need also creates more risk associated with delivery and adequacy of a purchase. In the BUYGRID formulation, a new purchase involves higher risk and so justifies a more-complete purchase process.

Thus risk is an important part of the analysis of situational factors. One can use risk as a separate segmentation variable, perhaps as a compilation of several or even many types of risk. Or one can use the other variables instead of risk. The appropriate approach is that which yields the most insight and the most-useful segmentation.

7

The Innermost Nest: Personal Characteristics

People have a major effect upon the purchase process in companies and thus upon the purchase decision. If individuals differ from one another, then personal characteristics are likely to offer a useful basis of segmentation. Although this level of the nest is most like consumer-goods marketing because it involves individuals, it is important to view the individuals in an organizational context.

Consumer marketers have used a rich variety of microsegmentation variables to analyze the end-use consumer and his or her buying processes. These include general personality inventories, buyers' self-concept differentials, cognitive styles, self-actualization, and the more general AIO (activity-interest-opinion) measures that have led to life-style, or psychographic, segmentation (Mehrotra and Wells 1977). For industrial marketers, though the field is not nearly so rich, there have been studies directed at helping them segment served markets on the basis of individual buyer characteristics. Other lessons can be drawn from investigations of organizational-buying behavior.

Unfortunately there is not enough useful information about the industrial buyer's decision process. This is an important omission, since as Webster and Wind (1972) have pointed out, "Understanding the buying decision-maker's decision-making process . . . can serve as an operational surrogate for all the other determinants of the organizational buyer's behavior" (p. 106). That is, decision-making processes are the conduit through which all other industrial-buying variables eventually flow to affect purchasing patterns.

Buyer-Seller Similarity

Evans (1963) offered some interesting empirical work on salesperson-customer interactions. Noting the much-replicated finding from psychology that individuals similar to each other in attitudes or personal characteristics tend to be attracted to each other more than are individuals who are dissimilar, Evans hypothesized that the more similar the parties in a seller-buyer dyad, the more likely a sale will occur. He tested this notion in a field study of life-insurance selling, where he recruited eighty-six experienced male agents from three companies. From each person he obtained samples of recent successful and unsuccessful sales attempts. All prospects were interviewed about their attitudes toward life insurance and life-insurance salespeople; demographics, personality, and other background characteristics were also obtained. In general, Evans found that insurance agents were more similar to the sold than to the unsold prospects on a broad variety of measures, including age. Sold prospects perceived themselves to be more similar to the salespeople, and liked them more, than did unsold prospects. Gadel (1964) found the same results for the salesperson-customer age variable in a study of over 20,000 life-insurance policies. The results were strongest for young salespeople and tended to diminish with increasing salesperson experience.

The principle of similarity to the customer is not limited to attitudes or background variables; rather it appears to be a pervasive one that includes behavior and experience. In a classic study, Brock (1965) employed students working in the paint section of a department store as field experimenters. The students attempted to persuade customers to purchase a brand of paint either more or less expensive than the kind the customer requested. The salesperson said that he had used the recommended paint on the job that was either similar or dissimilar to the application the customer faced. More customers purchased the recommended paint, irrespective of the price involved, when the salesperson had used it for a job similar to the one they were undertaking.

Finally, extending the similarity concept to expectations, Tosi (1966) investigated interactions between wholesale-drug salespersons and retail pharmacists. The pharmacists were asked their perceptions of the behavior of the salesperson with whom they regularly interacted and also their perceptions of how an ideal salesperson might behave. Tosi found that the more similarity between the pharmacist's perception of the ideal salesperson's behavior and his perceptions of the actual salesperson's behavior, the fewer competitive salespeople and suppliers the customer tended to deal with. However, this similarity did not net the saslesperson a larger share of the customer's business. Tosi does not explain this apparent discrepancy.

Generally, then, whether dealing with background variables like age, attitudinal variables like beliefs, perceptual variables like role expectations, or behavioral variables like sales presentation, the greater the similarity between the salesperson and the prospect, the higher the probability of a sale.

The implications for market segmentation are clear. The sales force should be tailored as much as possible to the people on whom it calls. This is perhaps one reason for the success of salespeople who came from the companies and industries on whom they call. Taken more broadly, there are company-wide implications. For example, if one market segment is defined as those companies in which management makes the purchase decision, a company with an older, experienced, up-scale sales force will be more effective than one with a sales force lacking these characteristics. In fact, the latter company might want consciously to avoid such a market segment. Companies with technical sales forces, using this reasoning, should either call on customers with technically oriented buyers, call on customers in which the technical function is powerful, or change its sales force so that at least some of its people can more productively relate to other types of customers.

Clearly there are practical limits to this approach. As a general concept, however, it seems very usable.

Motivation

According to Hill, Alexander, and Cross (1975), price, quality, and service from the supplier have been viewed as the primary rational industrial-buying motives, with availability of goods during periods of uncertain supply and reliability of the transaction flow important secondary motives. A number of investigators have challenged this view, noting that the nonrational or social aspects of industrial buying are equally important. Webster (1968a), for example, presented evidence that industrial buying is a joint function of the personal needs of purchasers for recognition and advancement and their social needs to satisfy those in the firm who will be the users of the purchased good. As Webster pointed out, these two sets of needs will interact to determine attention, which information the purchasing manager allows himself or herself to be exposed to (selective exposure), and which information he or she will remember, given attention and exposure (selective retention). There is a possibility of considering rational information only if all three of these social filters allow the sales presentation to pass through.

It is clear that an understanding of both rational and nonrational motives is important to vendors that would undertake the psychological segmentation possible at the innermost level of the nest. But how are the motives of individual buyers to be diagnosed?

As far as is known from psychological research, the basic rule of motivation is that all buyers (indeed, all salespeople and all people) either are acting selfishly or are trying to be selfish and make some error that prevents successful implementation of this goal (Bonoma and Zaltman 1981). The formal statement of this principle of self-interest is that buyers attempt to maximize their gains and minimize their losses, as they perceive them, from purchase situations. The self-interest principle is not a narrow and deprecatory view of people, especially as modified here.

Both differences in perceptions and the possibility of mistakes allow for much variance in purchasing behavior. What is rewarding to one buyer may be unrewarding to another. The errors made in marketing or selling decision making could be the subject of a monograph in itself. Here the concern will be with how buyers choose in their own self-interest rather than with buying mistakes.

Research into the psychology of decisions provides three findings useful to understanding buying motives:

1. Buyers act as if a complex product or service were decomposable into bundles of benefits. They then decide on these bundles. Examples are ease of operation, price, and the safety of a well-known vendor. Different buyers assign different subjective ratings to these benefits.
2. Buyers separate the set of bundles offered to them into various classes. The most-common separation is into financial, product-service feature, social-political, and personal-benefit classes. Each buyer ascribes a different importance to each class. For some buyers, the financial benefits of a contemplated purchase are paramount; for others, the social-political benefits of how others in the company will view the purchase. Of course, the dimensions may be related, as when getting the lowest-cost product (financial) results in good performance evaluations and a promotion (social-political).

3. Buyers ordinarily are not positive that purchasing the proposed product will actually result in the delivery of a desired benefit. Usually they are only more or less confident that the product or service will provide the desired quality. For example, a control computer sold on its reliability and industrial-strength construction may or may not fulfill that promise in service.

Applying the self-interest rule given what is known about how buyers see offerings, we can state generally what will happen during purchase deliberations. The buyer will act to maximize the value of the benefits offered weighted by his or her confidence that the promised benefit will actually be experienced if the purchase is made. Thus, well-known vendors may have some advantage with their claims of benefits over lesser-known companies, since buyers may be more confident that their claims have substance.

Not all promised benefits will be equally desired, however. Managers have top-priority benefit classes, and benefits in this class will be of more concern and value than others. For example, the decider who top ranks financial priorities may decide to risk possible service-reliability liabilities to obtain cost-reduction benefits. Another manager in the same company who is primarily concerned with reducing social-political risks should service problems arise may reach the opposite decision. Figure 7-1 shows the four benefit classes into which buyers partition benefits and gives some examples for each class using a telecommunications decision.

A simple analysis by vendor management that outlines how the central decision-makers in the buying company rank the four benefit classes, as well as guesses at how important various specific benefits are to the buyers, can have immense value to the selling company. The process of thinking through the motivational classes clarifies selling strategy and can lead to better tailoring of selling tactics to buyer motivations. If desired, a more-rigorous analysis can be undertaken where the values and certainty of each specific benefit are estimated in an attempt to pinpoint what the buyer will do. Such quantitative analyses are appropriate for national-account managers, where the stakes are high and the knowledge of the customer is often extensive. But for purposes of improved segmentation, it is the way of thinking in terms of buyer self-interest and matching company offerings to sought benefits that is important to the selling-company management.

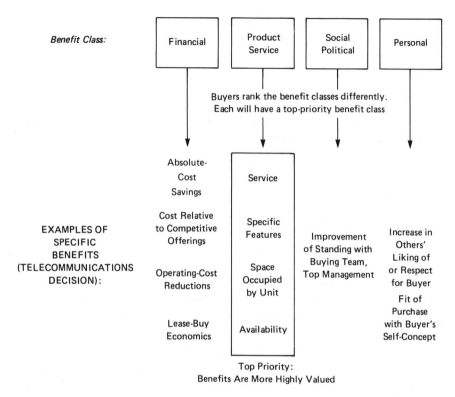

Figure 7-1. Overview of Dominant Buying Motives, by Benefit Class

The self-interest rule has important implications. It suggests that there is no easy way to understand what buyers want and will do, short of salespeople learning the field. The buying center must be identified, powerful decision makers culled, and intelligence gathered on the classes of benefits these decision makers regard as vital to making a purchase.

The motivation scheme suggests several leverage points for assessing and changing a buyer's motivations. The vendor can elect to focus the buyer's attention on benefits currently not fully considered. Or in a benefits-altering approach, sellers can act to deemphasize the buyer's desire for benefits on which the vendor's offering stacks up poorly and attempt to refocus the buyer's attention toward benefits on which the product does better. By refocus we do not mean changing what the buyer feels is important but providing new information that may lead to conclusions more favorable to the product. For example, a buyer may be concerned that a vendor's word processor does not have as much memory as a competitor's. If the vendor's equipment has special software to manage the flow of information from the machine to its disk drives, however, the memory-size difference may not have the importance to the buyer it originally assumed. Or approaching the selling situation from a confidence-altering point of view, the vendor can act to increase the buyer's certainty in the vendor's promised benefits compared to the competition's. Each of these strategies may require different selling tactics. Demonstrations of equipment are good confidence-raising tools, for example, while calculations of lease-purchase economics can help change benefit-value estimates.

Finally, it is often the case that vendors try to change what the buyer wants, or which class of benefit is top priority, by insisting that the buyer change his or her preferences while giving no good reasons to do so. Such an approach is almost always unsuccessful.

The implications of the psychological work on motivation are fairly clear for market segmentation: if the vendor cannot meet the basic needs of the buyers in a given segment, it is sensible not to enter that market. More positively, tailored communications programs can be developed to appeal to the motivations of different individuals in the buying organization. We can even picture tailored product, price, and distribution programs that meet the differing motivations of differing individuals, within practical and legal constraints.

Perception

In complex purchase situations where there are many buying influences, the powerful buyers invariably have a wide range of perceptions about the vending company. One buyer will have a friend at another company who has used a similar product and dislikes it. Another may have talked to someone who talked to someone with a similar product who claims that the vending company "even sent a guy out on a plane to Hawaii to fix the unit there quickly. These guys really care." Since humans are prone to making global judgments of liking and disliking on the basis of incomplete data, the question of how the buyers perceive the selling company, its products, and its personnel is of importance to effective segmentation.

Although there are scores of ways to talk about how managers perceive vendors' efforts, one simple scheme works quite well. This asks for management's best estimate of the important buyers' overall judgment of the vending company and its actions. A continuum can be used to record this judgment, ranging from totally negative through indifferent to totally positive:

$$|(-)----------(0)-----------(+)|$$
Negative   Neutral   Positive

If a more-complex segmentation is desired, selling management can place its products on one dimension and its company and people on another. Then buyer perceptions become judgments in a 2 x 2 space (see figure 7–2).

Different buying-center members have different perceptions. People from different functional areas, for example, can be expected to have different perceptions. Levitt (1967) had technical (nonpurchasing) as well as purchasing personnel, after exposure to either a good or a poor sales presentation, state whether they would recommend adoption of the product (a paint ingredient). The salesperson was represented as being from either a well-known or a lesser-known supplier firm. Levitt found that company reputation produced the expected effect of more customer endorsement for adoption, but only among the technical and not the purchasing personnel. He argued that it is possible that the purchasing agents become sophisticated with experience in evaluating company presentations and may tend to discount the rewarding effects of reputation because of this experience.

In an environment of scarce marketing resources, the highest investment in marketing communications should initially be made to reach those in the buying company favorably disposed toward the selling company's efforts. They are partially presold and represent a good selling wedge. In corporate jet selling, vendors often give separate demonstrations to pilots and to executives. If it is known that the chief executive officer is favorably disposed to the vendor or its product, it is usually better to conduct the executive demonstration first to create a champion for the product. Pilots' objections about landing requirements and fuel-consumption rates often melt away with the knowledge that their boss likes the plane. The reverse demonstration sequence works well when the pilots are known to be

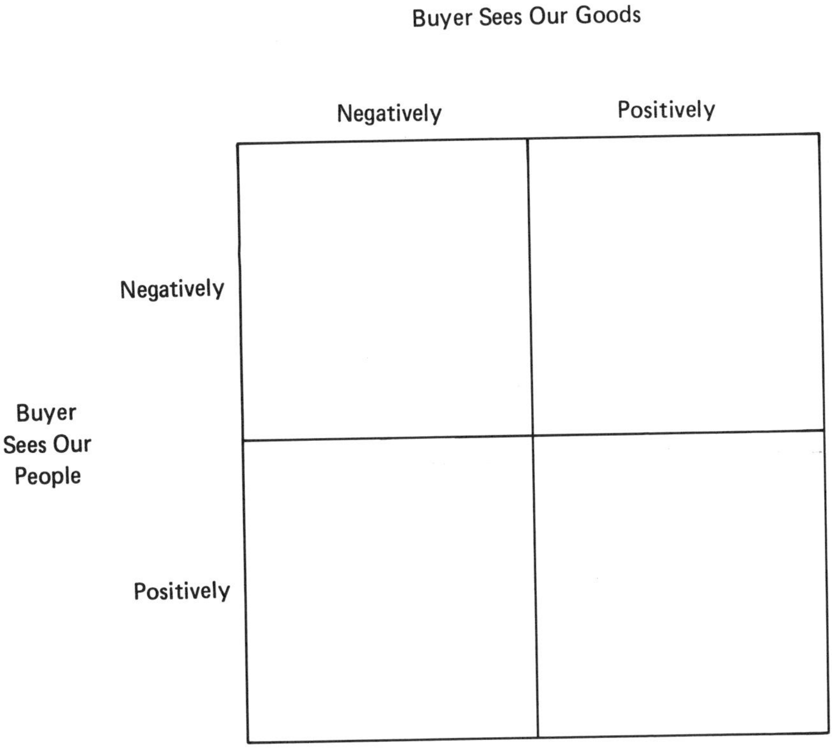

Buyer Sees Our Goods

Source: Adapted from T.V. Bonoma, "Major Sales: Who *Really* Does the Buying?" *Harvard Business Review* 61 (May–June 1982):118.

Figure 7-2. Matrixed Perceptual Space

favorable toward the vendor or its equipment and the executive uninterested. The goal of segmenting by positive perceptions of individual company personnel is to create champions in the buying company who will help to sell their colleagues.

Risk-Management Strategies

Many industrial-purchase situations involve substantial risks. The people doing the buying are subjected to a variety of organizational risks, including the risk due to the high impact poor performance or failure in service can have on a complex usage system. The whole system can be brought to a stop because of the failure or absence of even relatively minor materials, components, capital-equipment supplies, or services. The people who purchase must develop risk-management strategies. This section considers these strategies as a means of segmentation, a useful means for market selection and the development of tailored marketing programs, particularly communications programs. Risk-management strategies vary across personnel, company, and decision-specific factors, with accompanying implications for segmentation. In particular, risk-reduction activities are prevalent and important.

Wilson and his colleagues (Wilson 1971; Monoky, Mathews, and Wilson 1975; Wilson and Little 1971) have conducted a series of questionnaire-based investigations into purchasing decision making through which they have determined the prevalence of risk-averse purchasers. Wilson (1971) identified two major decision styles in purchasing behavior: normative and conservative. Normative choosers, who accounted for 30 percent of Wilson's sample, tried to maximize the economic expected value of purchases to their companies in a straightforward manner. Conversatives (55 percent of the sample), by contrast, did not make choices consistent with economic expected value but instead avoided uncertainty and the possibility of large negative outcomes; they were risk avoiders. A small third group switched between these strategies. As Wilson points out, an industrial salesperson can tailor a presentation to the decision style of the customer. Normative decision makers may be more influenced by economic arguments; conservative ones by reassurances about quality, delivery, and service or other risk-reducing messages.

Clearly the purchasing manager's reaction to risk is central for understanding and segmenting the purchasing situation. Wilson's evidence suggests strongly that buyers can be categorized as risk prone, risk neutral, or risk averse. The concept of risk (see Cox 1967) essentially may be taken to refer to an individual reaction to a choice situation in which either the probabilities of failure or the outcomes associated with failure are high. Risk-prone individuals act to seek out these settings; risk-averse individuals avoid them.

Selling folklore and other literature substantiate Wilson's finding that most purchasers are risk averse. (See Howard 1973 for a good managerial discussion of risk aversion in industrial buying.) Our observations suggest, moreover, that the buyers in some industries are more conservative and risk averse than in others. Slow-moving, stable industries tend to hire and breed managers who can afford to avoid risk, particularly if there is substantial inherent risk in their basic business. We would guess that the folklore about conservative bankers is founded in fact, because bankers rent a product that they then want returned. Other industries seem to hire and breed managers more willing to accept risk. High-fashion and high-technology industries require people with the ability to accept change and risk.

Nondominant suppliers who might offer more product benefit per dollar but greater risk and uncertainty are more likely to meet success in selling to the less-risk-averse people, companies, and industries. The usefulness of risk-management strategies as a segmentation variable extends beyond the simple separation of people and companies into risk avoiders and risk accepters. Risk perceptions have a major impact on the buying process.

Wilson, Mathews, and Sweeney (1971) administered a questionnaire to 130 members of the National Association of Purchasing Managers, asking them to evaluate two suppliers for electronic components. They identified four distinct risk-reduction patterns used by purchasers. The first, external uncertainty reduction, included strategies in which the buyer wanted to visit the cheaper supplier's plant or get a top-management commitment from the supplier about delivery. The second, internal uncertainty reduction, involved looking for published information about the suppliers, calling other buyers, and so on. The third strategy, external consequence reduction, involved negotiating with the supplier on price or splitting the order between suppliers. The fourth, internal consequence reduction, involved strategies in which the buyer consulted with his or her own management before making a decision. In other words, buyers differed as to where they gathered information (internal versus external) and the type of risk they attempted to lower. Some tried to lower uncertainty (the probability of failure) while others tried to lessen consequences (the outcome of failure).

Wilson, Mathews, and Sweeney's results have clear applicability for segmentation. For an established vendor of computer-room supplies who decides to bring out a line of computer peripherals, for example, their findings tell the company to partition its customers and prospects into two groups. In the first group will be current customers uncertain about the company's ability to produce hardware. These customers should be approached with trials, offers of plant visits, and so on. In the other group will be prospects who have never dealt with the vendor before but are attracted by the new hardware. An advertising campaign stressing the vendor's experience and reliability, or testimonials from satisfied users, may be required to attract them.

Cardozo (1968) also reported some findings on buyers' risk-reduction strategies. When dollar expenditures for a given purchase were high, a major element of risk was paying a premium price, and there was doubt about the supplier's ability to meet specifications, simultaneous scanning of purchasing alternatives was likely to be invoked; that is, several possible vendors were evaluated at the same time. On the other hand, when expenditures were low, risk of failure to meet purchase specifications was low, and the major risk was interruption of supply, sequential scanning of each alternative was more likely. That is, one vendor at a time would be evaluated, with the buyer stopping at the first acceptable supplier.

Firms can use Cardozo's findings in several ways to aid in segmentation. For example, a vendor can set its marketing mix, especially prices and terms, so as to encourage undesirable segments to look elsewhere for a vendor. Offering premium prices to prospective clients with low volumes or unexciting requests is routinely used by businesses with limited production capacities (such as, lawyers and consultants) to discourage this business and to leave room for more-attractive sales. By premium pricing or less-than-ideal terms, the vendor encourages simultaneous scanning, which Cardozo has identified as intensifying competition in risky purchases. The vendor can thus increase the risk to some purchasers, but not to others, within legal limits.

Cardozo (1968) reported that buyers appear to differ in their perception of different types of risk as more or less dangerous, and buyers differ in their self-confidence that they can manage one versus another kind of risk. For example, late delivery of raw materials is a risk that cannot be taken for a purchasing manager with automated mass-production site and low inventories, but the absence of a sufficient stock of spare parts for the machines may be viewed by the same buyer with apparent equanimity. The purchaser may be much more confident of being able to obtain equipment parts if needed and may thus find this risk more tolerable.

Cardozo has offered a list of six conditions for determining when purchase risk will be perceived as high:

1. The purchase dollar amount is large.
2. The purchase is complex.
3. The percentage of the total value added to the product by the purchasing firm is substantial.
4. The probability of the buyer's making an unsatisfactory choice appears high to him or her.
5. The consequences of making an unsatisfactory choice are highly visible.
6. The purchase may exert substantial influence on the market for the particular commodity.

Although Cardozo's listing is not a guide for determining the reaction of individual buyers to the various purchase dimensions, it does suggest that purchase situation may be a major determinant of when buyers will act in a risk-averse fashion, though there is some evidence that individuals have generalized risk-management styles that they apply across many situations. Chapter 6 spoke of risk as a situational variable in the purchase process. Combining the concept of the individual's response to risk with the risk inherent in the particular purchase situation leads to the scheme shown in figure 7–3.

Under low-risk situations we believe that buyers generally will behave as if they were risk neutral and will try to maximize the product of the worths they assign to the benefits and the probability that they will actually receive these benefits if they make the purchase. It is only when the potential effects of a wrong choice are high and visible (the right-hand column in figure 7–3) that the individual's attitude toward risk becomes important. At that point, it becomes a useful segmentation variable. Then a vendor can develop segmented communication strategies to help the more risk-averse prospects manage their risk. The vendor may even target a different communications mix to different personnel or groups within the firm based on their response to risk.

Personal-Characteristics Nest

There is a clear use for individual-buyer analysis in industrial marketing; however, there may be serious problems with some applications of psychological segmentation in everyday practice. While

Level of Risk in Situation

		Low	High
	Highly Risk Averse[a] Moderately		
Response of Individual to Risk	Risk Neutral		
	Risk Seeking		

[a]Because risk aversion seems to be so common, we subdivided it into high and moderate categories.

Figure 7-3. Risk as Related to Individuals and Situations

segments based on psychology may be useful and perhaps even profitable, it is difficult, if not impossible, to pre-identify individual buyers based on characteristics such as high self-confidence or risk aversion. Individuals do not wear tags asserting their psychological makeup and probably would not submit to detailed diagnostic measurements. Thus segmentation on psychological grounds is difficult to apply other than to current customers and some prospects whom the marketer has observed personally. The quality of the analysis depends upon the sales force's ability to understand and appreciate the subtle signals sent by customers and prospects in day-to-day interaction. This, of course, implies that only a well-trained sales force sensitive to individual differences can gather the necessary data in most situations. There may be other situations, probably quite infrequent, where a survey of people involved in the decision process can be performed. Although a rare occurrence, the thought is an intriguing one. Such a survey might help a company to understand better the kinds of risk that its buyers perceive, their motivations, and their perception of the seller, its products, and services. Certainly Moriarty's research (1980) shows the methodology of doing such a survey and proves the feasibility.

Some companies undoubtedly will learn how to orient their communications programs toward specific concerns of segments of the market. Such communications might be of little interest to other segments and thus not harmful to the company's approach to those other segments. If the company measures the response to its advertising, it should carefully differentiate the response of the targeted segment from the response of the nontargeted segments. Media, such as direct mail and catalogs, that can be directed to more-specific audiences may lessen possible confusion and waste through overlap. With careful analysis and creative formulation of tailored marketing plans and programs, the marketing executive can make use of the innermost nest, personal characteristics.

8 Applying Market-Segmentation Schemes

Approaches to Segmentation

Whether a nested approach is used or not, there are two distinct ways in which an industrial marketer can segment a market. One approach emphasizes segmentation based upon customer needs and works from the customer toward the vendor. This approach is similar in effect to benefit segmentation in the consumer-goods field as suggested by Haley (1968). The goal of the marketing strategy is to provide the specific products that generate benefits to meet the needs of chosen market segments. (We use the word *product* to mean the total bundle of benefits that the customer receives, including physical-product attributes and services.) Each segment will be made up of customers (or potential customers) with a common set of needs. In theory, the needs of the customers in one segment will differ from those in other segments. The advantage of this approach is that it segments the market by the most-important variable: customer needs. That, after all, is the basis on which customers make choices. It is thus theoretically sound, but it is not always easy to implement, and in some situations it is impossible to implement.

The second approach works outward from the selling company and segments the market in ways related to identifiability and accessibility. All of the members of a segment can be identified in the same way and are accessible through the same means. Ease of implementation is the strongest advantage of this approach.

Several examples will help explain the concepts. Almost every market has customers who are able and willing to purchase a basic product without optional features and attributes and without adjunct services. They want the cheapest product at the cheapest price. Clearly buyers in this price-sensitive segment differ from buyers in other segments on the basis of benefits or needs. But it is often difficult and sometimes impossible to identify price-sensitive buyers without a careful and expensive personal selling campaign.

91

Buyers who attend a particular trade show might, on the other hand, be defined as a market segment. Certainly they are identifiable and accessible by the same means: attendance at the trade show. But it is likely that they do not share the same specific needs. Further, some buyers who attend the show are likely to share needs with some buyers who do not.

The needs or benefits-oriented segmentation approach is more attractive in a theoretical sense but is not as easily implemented as the identifiable-accessible approach. Sometimes the two approaches can be made to coincide, a fortuitous event. Figure 8–1 shows the difference between the inward and outward orientation of the two approaches and where an overlap is encountered. Where the two approaches coincide, the customers in a particular segment share a common need and are identifiable and accessible through a common approach. Thus the segmentation approach is sound and implementable.

Before moving on to the economics of applying market-segmentation schemes, it is useful to look at the benefits and applicability of each of the two distinct forms of segmentation. Table 8–1 summarizes the role that the two types of segmentation can play in each task or program that a marketing organization must perform. The table shows that, by and large, those tasks related to the manufacture of the product—product policy, price, and to a lesser extent, perhaps, market selection—can make especially good use of the needs-benefits segmentation. Those tasks, on the other hand, that generally relate to communication—advertising, distribution policy, and personal selling—can make good use of the identifiable-accessible approach. Two tasks can make equal use of both approaches: personal selling and distribution. These deserve further discussion.

On the first sales call, personal selling is like advertising. It is aimed at a target audience that may or may not be in an appropriate segment in terms of needs. It is, however, possible to select an identifiable-accessible marketing segment for salespeople to call on. After the first contact, the salesperson can separate prospects (and existing customers, of course) on the basis of their needs. The personal-selling task thus changes from using primarily the identifiable-accessible approach to using the needs-benefits approach. One advantage of personal selling as a communication medium is that a salesperson can segment the market at the most-disaggregate level: that of an individual buying influence.

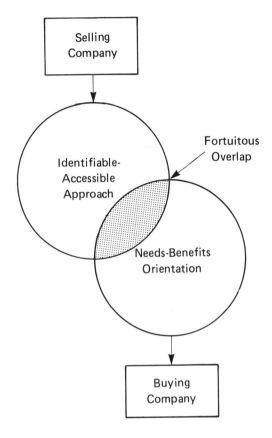

Figure 8-1. Two Approaches to Segmentation

Table 8-1
Basis of Segmentation

Task	Customer Driven: Needs-Benefit Segmentation	Company Driven: Identifiable-Accessible Approach
Analysis	Difficult but important	Easy
Market selection	Applicable	Sometimes applicable
Product policy	Applicable	Not applicable
Pricing	Applicable	Not applicable
Personal selling	Applicable after interaction	Applicable for initial call
Advertising	Applicable in some situations	Applicable
Distribution policy	Applicable	Applicable

A distributor performs a variety of functions that relate to communication and product policy (in the broad sense), including: communication (including display and personal selling), inventory support and physical distribution (related to product policy, provides location and time utility), credit (related to product policy and pricing), and postsales service (related to product policy).

In thinking about distribution policy as it relates to the communications function, it is natural to begin with the identifiable-accessible segmentation approach. One might, for example, use a particular distributor to reach customers in Wyoming or consider the use of distributors for small customers while serving large end users and OEMs through a direct sales force (Boston Consulting Group, n.d.). Because distribution policy also affects product policy in areas such as inventory support and postsales service, however, it is also necessary to consider needs-benefit segmentation.

Looking at the differences between needs-benefits segmentation and identifiable-accessible segmentation in terms of their impact on the different marketing tasks helps to clarify the immense value of having a segmentation scheme that does both. The identifiable-accessible approach works well with communication, and the needs-benefits approach works well with product policy and price. (It is interesting that consumer-goods marketers tend to bring together the needs-benefits approach and the identifiable-accessible approach because the intangible benefits, such as prestige, developed through promotion are so much a part of product policy.) If the two segmentation approaches can overlap (as in figure 8–1), then product policy, pricing, communication, and distribution can be brought close together into a coherent marketing strategy.

Economics of Applying Market Segmentation

Market segmentation is not an inexpensive process. There are costs in gathering the data necessary to segment a market effectively and costs in developing and implementing strategies, plans, and programs that relate to each market segment. In fact, some authors argue that segmentation costs are now so high that it can be profitable for firms deliberately not to segment in some cases (Resnin, Turner, and Mason 1979). This section considers three aspects of the economics of market segmentation: how does the amount of segmentation affect the cost of segmentation; how does the marketing mix for each segment (the seller's response to each segment) affect the economics of segmentation; and how do different characteristics of the segments affect the cost of doing business in the segment?

Segmentation Costs

Gathering the data that form the basis for market segmentation is expensive. It involves the variable costs of hiring market-research firms to collect the data, as well as the fixed costs related to the direct and overhead costs of the executives who hire and manage the market-research firms, or an equivalent in-house operation, and who analyze the data so that decisions can be made about the best way to segment the market.

Another group of costs is incurred in the development of strategies, plans, and programs to approach each separate segment. These, too, involve the costs of administrative effort and then the cost of developing products, pricing schedules, advertising programs, and specialized sales forces aimed at each segment. Products that meet the needs of one segment are unlikely to be as appropriate for another, and the same is true for all other elements of the marketing plan.

A third cost is that of implementing the different programs and monitoring their effectiveness. For example, if the strategy of the firm is built around a strong and specialized sales presence in each of several industries, each segment must have its own sales force, which will require specialized recruiting, training, and sales aids. The salespeople representing each sales force in a given territory may overlap, increasing travel time and expense. The same is true, perhaps to a much greater degree, in the factory. Often each user segment must have its own product line with attendant duplication of facilities and efforts. Managing the efforts of such a multiproduct, multisales force operation is expensive. Administrative costs and the costs from low economies of scale can be substantial.

The benefits of segmentation in terms of additional sales volume, added economies of scale, and marginal profits must justify the added cost of segmentation. As the number of segments approached separately increases, the administrative costs probably increase more quickly. As the size of each additional segment decreases, the likelihood of a profitable approach to the segment probably also decreases, although the exact shape of the curve will depend a great deal on the nature of the production process, the degree of standardization in components, and other manufacturing, marketing, and administrative factors.

The important point here is that it costs a great deal of money to segment a market. Further, as the degree of segmentation (perhaps measured by differences among segments) and the number of segments served increase, the cost increases.

Segmentation Economics and the Marketing Mix

The cost of segmentation is closely related to the type of approach a marketer makes toward a segmented market. Some parts of the marketing mix are cheaper to differentiate than others. Figure 8–2 gives a sense of the differences in direct cost for four different marketing tasks. The cheapest of the four to implement is market selection. After the data related to segmentation are collected and analyzed, marketing management decides to approach certain segments or not to approach them. The direct cost of selecting a segment for approach is fairly low and mainly involves executive and administrative functions. Notice, however, that there may also be opportunity

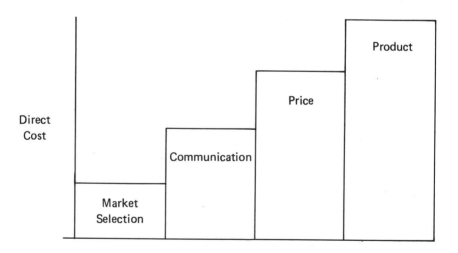

Figure 8–2. Direct Cost of Use of Market Segmentation

costs—for example, of neglecting a particular segment that might in fact be highly profitable.

The next least-expensive task is to develop tailored communication approaches for different market segments. It is fairly inexpensive to develop and execute a specialized advertising campaign for a specific segment of an industrial market. (The impact may not be great either.) More expensive, but still relatively inexpensive compared to specialized pricing and products, is the cost of organizing and deploying a specialized sales force. The one general exception might be markets that are communications intensive rather than production intensive, meaning simply that more cost is accounted for by the communication function than by the production function. There are not many such markets in the industrial sector, but there are some, such as high-quality nuts and bolts used for repair and maintenance.

Further up the scale of expense are specialized pricing programs. These programs are hard to administer, particularly when product differences are not present. They are also expensive in terms of the margin given up through price cuts. For example, volume discounts for large orders can easily run 20 to 40 percent, much greater than the added cost of a specialized sales force.

By far the most-expensive approach toward a segmented market is a specialized product line. Large sums of money are needed to develop, test, and introduce specialized products. Such products wreak havoc in a production facility, forcing short runs, constant retraining of labor, limited automation, increased inventories, and general disorganization. On the other hand, customers with unique needs are most responsive to the unique benefits of a specialized product line.

In a sense, then, figure 8–2 also reflects the potential impact of a specialized program on a target-market segment, with communication, particularly advertising, having the smallest impact on the segment and specialized pricing and product policy having the greatest impact. The cost of making changes in the product line for special segments is closely related to the nature of the production process and the degree of standardization possible in different products.

Figure 8–3 combines the two concepts discussed so far in this section: the relationship between segmentation economics and the degree of segmentation, and the direct costs of the marketing tools

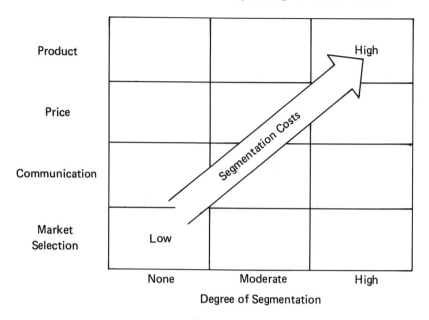

Figure 8–3. Direct Cost of Segmentation

used to approach a segmented market. Toward the top and right of the figure, the direct cost of segmentation increases.

It is possible to think of the market-selection, communications, pricing, and product approaches to market segmentation as fitting into a nest much like that used to describe the different forms of segmentation in chapter 2. The basis for this approach is that one should, for a given situation, use the cheapest marketing tool possible. Thus if one can adequately approach a market segment with a specialized advertising program, one might not resort to a specialized price program. Figure 8–4 shows the four approaches as a set of nested boxes, with the most-expensive nest, specialized product policy, at the center. The marketing executive should move from the outside to the inside only as justified by the expected rewards of such a policy versus the higher cost.

Figure 8–4 also provides a good way in which to discuss distribution. Distribution cuts across communication, price, and product policy because when a distributor is chosen, the manager inevitably gives up some, and sometimes all, control over the marketing mix in favor of the distributor's choices on product policy, pricing, and

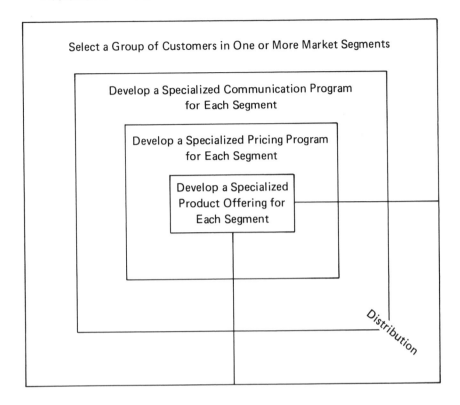

Figure 8-4. A Nested Scheme of Approaches toward a Segmented Market

communications. Distribution can be used as a response to the special needs of a particular segment with regard to either communication, price, or product, although often they come as one package. Thus if the seller wants to use distribution in a segmented approach to communication, it is often forced to take a segmented approach to pricing and product policy as well. Because a particular form of distribution can define all three levels of response to segmentation, and in doing so also influence market selection, distribution is depicted as a sector of the diagram in figure 8-4. It clearly needs special treatment and understanding.

Cost of Serving Each Segment

To this point, it has been shown that the direct costs of segmentation are a function of the degree of segmentation and the marketing approach used in responding to the needs of the segments. A third factor that enters into the cost of segmentation is the choice of particular market segments. To consider the issue of which market segments to approach, it is necessary to introduce the concept of efficiency. Efficiency is a measure of the number of good potential customers that exist for the product in each market segment, divided by the size of the segment. In essence, efficiency is related to the density of good prospects among the population of the market segment.

To clarify the concept, let us use the example of a producer of small safes. At one time, the president of the company said, "I don't care whether the customer is a small business with critical records or an old person with a photo of a dead spouse to protect. We want to sell to everyone." Figure 8–5 shows why it might not be equally profitable for this safe company to pursue certain segments of the market for small safes. Clearly the density functions of potential customers who need or want a small safe (and for whom the safe produced by this particular company is a good match in terms of benefits, such as size and price) differ among the four segments shown. The "people with photos" segment, though its total size is a massive 16.1 million (these figures are hypothetical), provides a poor density function of only 2 prospects per 100,000 individuals. On the other hand, professional corporations of lawyers, doctors, and so on, provide a high-density function of 50 good prospects per 100,000, though the entire segment is much smaller than the first.

As in this example, many companies must choose from among several market segments the most-advantageous ones to approach. Density is an important criterion because it is directly related to communications efficiency; high-density functions enable marketers to get more results from a limited communications budget.

It is also worth mentioning two other important criteria. One is the degree of fit between the product-service bundle that the company offers and the needs of the customers in the segment. Clearly the better the fit, the greater the likelihood of making sales with a large percentage of the segment population. As the likelihood of sales goes up, the profit potential from penetrating the segment goes up too. The second criterion is the difference between the needs of a prospective segment and that of an already-served segment. Because companies over time develop sets of well-honed skills to meet specific needs, the closer the needs of each new market segment are to

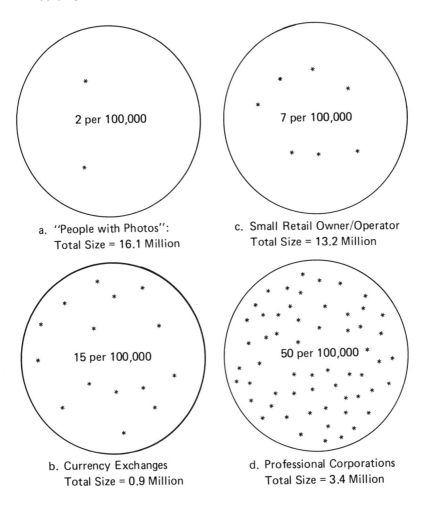

Figure 8-5. Four Potential Customer-Density Plots for Small Safes

those of the existing served segment(s), the easier it is for the company to approach the new segment and the more likely it is that the approach will be profitable.

In practice, the most-common market-selection error made by managers is an error of resolve. Management can find it hard to turn down business that does not fit the company's strategic choice. Especially in businesses where there is a high proportion of fixed costs (as with airlines), low marketing to total costs (industrial chemicals), or strong market cyclicality (construction), there is a strong tendency to take any business to cover the cost base or the slow periods. The danger, of course, is that more-profitable prospects will go begging because capacity is filled with low-profit customers, and that price cutting by individual companies leads to general price degradation. One manufacturer of prestressed concrete, for example, managed a backlog target closely in order to assure itself of continuous production economies. In slow times, the sales force would greatly increase its efforts to keep up the backlog. Prices were shaved to marginally profitable or sometimes no-profit levels to encourage customers to buy. As times improved, the firm repeatedly found its order backlogs long and was unable to offer the attractive deliveries that would allow it to book as much high-profit business as was available.

We are not suggesting that the firm's market-selection scheme should be inflexible or that cost-covering business should be refused in slack times. However, management must resolutely assess what will be gained (profit) and what future opportunities may be lost (costs) when making a decision to serve a customer. Sometimes the best answer is "no."

The Optimum Point

The direct cost of segmenting a market increases depending on the nature of the company's approach to its market segments (as measured by the marketing mix tailored to each segment and the amount of tailoring done). The direct cost of segmenting a market increases as the number of individual segments served increases. These two cost factors are combined in the direct-cost curve of figure 8–6. Correspondingly the opportunity cost of not serving each additional segment decreases with increasing segmentation effort, assuming that the most-profitable segments are served first. This is shown in figure 8–6 by the opportunity-cost curve, which falls from left to right.

The shape of the two curves is important. The opportunity-cost curve falls at a decreasing rate as the amount of segmentation increases because each new segment to be approached is smaller and offers less profit potential (or if neglected, less opportunity cost). Also because the segments are being approached by increasingly less-effective means, the profit potential (or the opportunity loss if

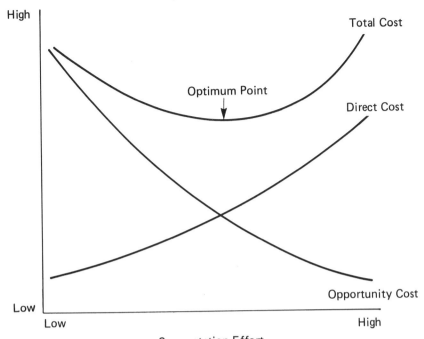

Figure 8-6. Segmentation Cost Curves

neglected) is again increasingly limited. The direct-cost curve, on the other hand, accelerates at an increasingly rapid rate because of the same phenomena.

The result, we believe, if opportunity and direct costs are added together to yield total cost and graphed as in figure 8–6, is a parabolic shape to the total cost curve. Although we do not know whether the curve is a steep or shallow parabola or just where the optimum point is, we believe the concept is solid. In every market at any given time, there is an optimum degree of segmentation. This speculation deserves further research.

Applying Segmentation Schemes

The existing segmentation literature largely ignores the matter of implementation. Chapter 1 addressed implementation of the nested approach in terms of both segmentation economics and segmentation by element of the marketing mix. These analyses led to a second nest (figure 8–4), relating segmentation tools and economics, and to a notion of optimal segmentation (figure 8–6). We believe the results of these analyses can serve as a guide to the manager needing to make applied segmentation decisions.

There are two rules for managerially applying the nested approach:

1. The nests should be investigated only deeply enough for useful segmentation to result. The manager should not look at personal factors, for example, if demographic variables will do. Segmentation is too expensive to allow random exploration in the nests without clear purpose. Where exploration must occur, it should start from the outer level and move to the inner-nest levels only if necessary.
2. The best way to identify economically feasible segments is through creative thinking about the customer base, perhaps using the simple diagrammatic matrixes presented in chapter 2. The more preliminary work done, the more economical and useful the resulting scheme is likely to be. Usefulness should always dominate elegance in this thinking.

With these reminders on how to use the nested approach, the guidelines from this chapter will allow effective segmentation implementation. If the steps recommended are omitted, even the best implementation efforts will fail.

9

Controlling Segmentation Implementation

If a company is to be effective at approaching a market in a segmented fashion, management must have a way to determine the profitability of each segment currently served and to assess the likely profitability of potential new segments. Without such data it is impossible to manage current business or to make informed judgments about future business. Particularly problematic under such circumstances are decisions about which unserved segments to approach.

Much of the literature on information and control is excellent and directly applicable to segmentation (see Beik and Buzby 1973; Pokempner 1973; and Stephens 1972). Two areas of critical importance for segmentation control are what we will call customer-conversion analysis and segment-profitability analysis.[1] Customer-conversion analysis compares various segments in terms of the numbers of customers each will yield. Segment-profitability analysis, which is really good account management at the segment level, evaluates the quality of each customer generated from the segment.

Customer-Conversion Analysis

Figure 9-1 shows an inverted triangle that represents a scheme for evaluating current segments or computing the attractiveness of prospective ones. The control measures to be computed on each segment include density, efficiency, qualification, trial conversion, and repeat conversion.

The top of figure 9-1 shows that the manager starts with a group of prospects or customers that he or she is satisfied comprise a valid segment. Choices about which variables from the nest to employ for segmentation have already been made, as have decisions of how to approach each segment.

Given a potential or currently served segment the first step is to compute its density of prospects. The objective is to seek segments with the highest possible prospect density. A percentage measure

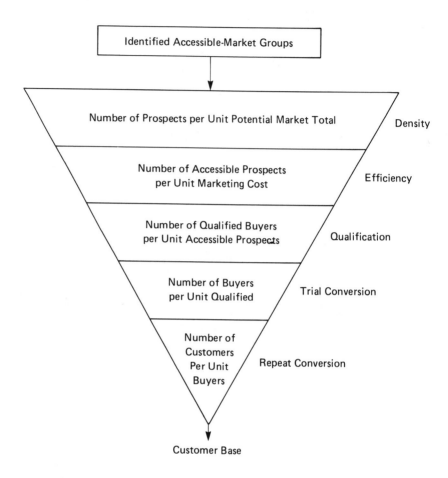

Note: Customer conversion is a joint function of density, efficiency, qualification, trial conversion, and repeat conversion.

Figure 9-1. Customer-Conversion Analysis

should be used to control for different absolute numbers of firms and prospects in each segment. For example, if market assessment indicates that thirteen of thirty-nine major industrial-supply houses are potential prospects for a vendor's computerized inventory-management service, the density of the segment equals 13/39, or 33 percent.

Computing the ability of the vending firm to access the potential-prospect list is the next customer-conversion-control measure. This measure asks how many of the total possible prospects (some call them "suspects" at this early marketing stage) can be reached per unit marketing cost. Prospect efficiency can be expressed as this ratio or more qualitatively as low, medium, or high marketing costs per prospect accessed. In a personal selling task, the location of the prospects will be a major factor in determining the sales force costs that would be incurred to reach each prospect.

The next conversion-control measure is either an estimate or actual figures on how many of the accessible prospects can be qualified for the purchase under consideration. In many businesses, qualification is not an issue; in others it is of maximal importance. Consider the selling task for business jets in the $3 million to $5 million range. Although many companies in the United States might correctly be thought of as prospects and most of them as accessible prospects, a much-smaller percentage will be qualifiable. Relevant qualifying variables in this industry include the geographical dispersion of the prospect's operating facilities. If the range of a business jet allows serving many of the prospect's operating units more efficiently or more quickly than with a comparable propeller plane, the prospect is more qualified. Traditional qualifying variables in many industries include buyer interest, Dun & Bradstreet rating, size of prospect, and proximity to a vendor service unit. However the criteria for qualification are chosen, the percentage of prospects that can be qualified for purchase (of the total number of prospects) is a useful segmentation control variable.

The essential difference between the density measure at the top of the triangle and the qualification measure is that qualifying a prospect will probably require some customer contact to assess buyers' interest and ability to buy. Density is the coarse screen of buying possibility; qualification the finer one of buying probability.

Trial conversion refers to the percentage of qualified prospects that can be persuaded to try or buy the vendor's product or service once. This makes them not customers but only trial users. For example, word-processing stations cost $7,000 to $15,000 each and have semicustom software. The preferred way to evaluate such machines in major corporations is to select one department or division of the firm to test a vendor's units. Thus an initial purchase of five to one hundred machines is often made, costing upward of $50,000. Yet the vendor who believes that by this sale it has converted the entire corporation to a loyal user may be greatly surprised when the user firm has completed its evaluation. Making the first sale does not yield a customer but only a trier. The first sale, however, is a necessary step in gaining customers, and the user-conversion measure computes the incidence of first sales for management analysis.

Finally, the astute manager will measure repeat conversion, or the percentage of users who become customers through repeated purchases. The higher this percentage, the more attractive the segment for pursuit.

The customer-conversion analysis suggested here can be used for a number of useful diagnostics. Abnormally low density among some current segments might indicate poor market selection. If efficiency is lower than desired, the manager can examine the market-communications methods currently employed to reach prospects, the marketing and sales force costs, or the mix of identified prospects in order to determine the source of the inefficiency. If qualification is unsatisfactory, either market-selection or -qualification procedures are called into question. If trial conversion is not at desired levels, the manager might look to the selling efforts and to the product or service delivered to ensure that both are adequate and offering desired benefits to prospects. If customer conversion is low, both the selling effort and the product-service mix may be possible causes.

Segment-Profitability Analysis

In addition to finding segments that generate a high customer-conversion ratio, it is necessary to obtain customers that can be serviced at a reasonable cost, can be maintained without excessive marketing expenditures, and hence can contribute a high margin to fixed business costs and profit. If other segments are capable of delivering a similar or greater amount of profit for less cost, it is clear that the manager will want to investigate more fully the economics and capabilities necessary to serve their needs.

Figure 9-2 presents an upward-pointing triangle that represents some notions about controlling segment profitability. The input to the top of the triangle is a market segment, and the first two sections deal with order size and product mix. If the customers the firm has attracted provide orders that cannot be filled profitably or if their product mix results in suboptimal utilization of resources, then

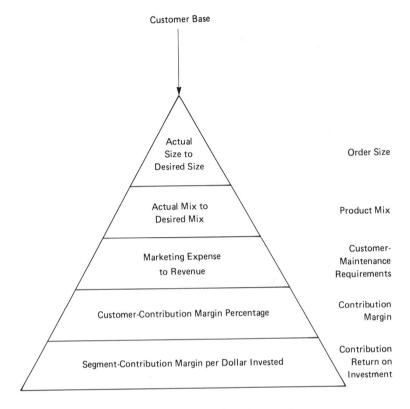

Figure 9–2. Segment-Profitability Analysis

the manager can question the desirability of serving the segment. For example, small electrical contractors often buy a wide range of products but in small quantities. This small-quantity, wide-variety order may be the foundation of the local industrial distributor's business but the bane of the larger distribution company, which primarily wholesales to other distributors but maintains counter service to contractors as well. Indeed it is not uncommon for firms that have made the analysis to report that such an order costs more to pick and fill than it returns to the vendor in contribution.

Desirable order sizes and product mixes depend not only on marketing costs but on production technology, distribution systems, and other variables. For example, in a business that uses a continuous-manufacturing process, low-demand specialty items are relatively unprofitable in periods of high demand because the changeover time interrupts the mill's long runs (which generate a more-limited variety of products in higher volumes and thus high dollar profits per hour of machine time). In tool and diemaking businesses, where a specialty-job-shop atmosphere prevails, a conceptually similar but opposite problem is sometimes encountered with regard to order size. Ambitious firms that have sold diligently to obtain large, batch-type orders have often found that they cannot deliver them at a profit because their marketing, production technology, and other business systems were set up to deal with low-volume, short-run items.

Regardless of the particular conditions, every business will have some optimal order size and desired product mix that returns maximum contribution dollars. It is suggested in figure 9-2 that periodically the manager should compare customer order sizes to the desired order size to ensure that either they are meeting order and mix criteria or there has been a conscious management decision to serve customers that do not meet the criteria. For example, a company may choose to service customers that individually do not meet the product-mix criterion but as a group generate a desirable product-mix portfolio.

The third section of the triangle in figure 9-2 turns from customer-serving costs to customer-maintenance costs. Continuing business from a customer ordinarily requires the investment of additional marketing resources, and different customers differ in the resources they require per dollar volume generated. Among the measures of marketing expense to revenue are, the costs of communication, the costs of price promotion (discounting and so on) and other costs per customer per unit time (usually a business quarter or year). Nonmonetary measures also exist, including total selling person-days per customer account in cases where large customers are involved and the sale is project oriented in nature (for example, major power-plant construction or amount of customer-applications engineering needed). Regardless of the particular measure chosen, the objective should be to compute the marketing costs involved in customer maintenance for each account and for each class of accounts treated as a segment.

Customer-contribution margin is another element of segment-profitability analysis. Order size, product mix, and marketing expense to sales-revenue measures all help determine a percentage contribution per revenue dollar for each segment. In essence, this is a measure of the amount of contribution available for covering fixed costs and providing profit after direct production, service, distribution, and marketing expenses are deducted. Analysis of contribution margin can be performed by account or market segment.

For the final step in the profitability analysis, contribution margins must be related to the investment cost of serving each account or segment. Often marketers find it difficult, if not impossible, to allocate investment to segments. Yet for larger segments (see Schiff and Schiff 1976) or key accounts, it is usually possible to get a good sense of the investment intensity required to service the segment. If this can be done, at least for the firm's major segments, it is possible to compute a rough but useful marketing return-on-investment ratio, which is the highest form of the control system we propose. Only by continually driving toward such an investment measure can the manager make well-reasoned decisions.

Two levels of aggregation have been mentioned: the individual-customer level and the segment level. Whenever possible, it is preferable to compute measures on the basis of individual customer accounts, as this allows decisions to be made on the customer level rather than on the segment level. However, the ultimate purpose is to gain information on segments, and the manager with no other information available might choose to analyze profitability at the segment level for all the measures, realizing the risk of retaining poor accounts with the good ones or abandoning good accounts in an otherwise-unattractive segment. The development of precise segments (for example, rural accounts, direct accounts, small accounts, urgent needs) can improve the quality of analysis.

Integration of the Measures

It is no accident that the customer-conversion triangle in figure 9-1 points down and the segment-profitability triangle in figure 9-2 points up. We feel strongly that the segment-control process requires the marketer first to explore customer-conversion analysis from the accessible market groups through to the customer base and then to track the profitability of the customer base through to the segment contribution to return on investment. Segmentation control can thus be thought of as forming an hourglass model that tracks the costs of getting customers and the return they deliver to the firm. Although managers can implement one or the other of the triangles separately, optimum results come from using them together.

10 Concluding Remarks

Although the purpose of this book is to take some of the guesswork out of the task of industrial-market segmentation through the provision of solid concepts and guidelines for implementation, industrial market segmentation is not an automatic, mechanical process. It requires a thorough understanding of the customer and prospect base, difficult choices about which segments will be approached and with what methods, and continual monitoring for success.

Perhaps the strongest advantage of the nested approach to segmentation is that it encourages clear and meticulous thinking by naming and ordering the various bases that managers can use to think about their markets. The nested approach stands up well to both of the tests we applied to it. First, it seems to organize much of what is currently known about industrial buyers that is relevant to segmentation in a manner that permits the marketing executive to understand and apply its levels usefully. Second, it serves as well to suggest several important segmentation nests where little is known. The operating and situational factors nests are the two primary examples. Further, the major advantages of the nests remain, and their importance is underscored by the literature review. The advantages are to order the ways in which markets can be segmented from most easily observable, or least intimate, to least easily observable, or most intimate, and to provide the segmentation effort with sequence as well as sense.

It is important to think through not only each nest but also the relationship of the variables in one nest to those in another. The inner, situational nest, for example, is in part defined by the interaction of several of the outer nests, which together create unique purchase situations. Conversely it is difficult to understand the purchasing situation or (to take a much more-visible nest) the purchasing approach of the firm without some understanding of the people doing the buying. Perhaps the clearest lesson to be gained from thinking through the nests is that selling and buying in industrial marketing are interrelated and interdependent. The manager who

113

would sell well, and segment customers effectively, must understand the buying process.

Finally, effective industrial market segmentation is not just a matter of careful thinking about the nests or of scrupulous selection of marketing tools (such as product and price) to carry out a segmented approach, or even of the institution of rigorous control measures to see how well a segmentation scheme is working. It is, rather, all three of these elements applied in a disciplined and creative manner by knowledgeable management.

Endnotes

Chapter 2

1. This concept was developed by our colleague Barbara B. Jackson.

2. Four good sources for consumer-goods segmentation are Woodside, Sheth, and Bennett (1977), particularly pp. 35–76; Frank, Massy, and Wind (1972); Engel, Fiorillo, and Cayley (1972); *Journal of Marketing Research* (August 1978), "Special Section: Market Segmentation Research," pp. 315–412; Scotton and Zallocco (1980).

3. One company with which we are familiar chose not to approach municipal governments (a major group of prospects for its product line) because of the low level of integrity its managers believed existed in municipal government buying units.

Chapter 5

1. Much of this section has been adapted from Bonoma (1982).

Chapter 9

1. Our colleague Rowland Moriarty has developed two categories conceptually similar to ours and has graciously shared his thinking with us.

Bibliography

Arndt, Johan. "Toward a Concept of Domesticated Markets." *Journal of Marketing* 43:4 (Fall 1979):69–75.

Banville, G.R. and Dornoff, R.J. "Industrial Source Selection Behavior—An Industry Study." *Industrial Marketing Management* 2:3 (June 1973).

Bauer, R.A. "Consumer Behavior as Risk Taking." In R.S. Hancock, ed., *Dynamic Marketing for a Changing World*, pp. 389–398. (Chicago: American Marketing Association, 1960).

Beik, Leland L., and Buzby, Stelphen L. "Profitability Analysis by Market Segment." *Journal of Marketing* 37 (July 1973):48–53.

Bellizzi, J.A. "Product Type and the Relative Influence of Buyers in Commercial Construction." *Industrial Marketing Management* 8 (June 1979):218–220.

Bonoma, T.V. "Major Sales: Who *Really* Does the Buying?" *Harvard Business Review* 61 (May–June 1982):111–119.

Bonoma, T.V. and Johnston, Wesley. "The Social Psychology of Industrial Buying and Selling." *Industrial Marketing Management* 17 (1978):213–224.

Bonoma, T.V., and Johnston, W.J. "Purchase of Capital Equipment and Industrial Service." *Industrial Marketing Management* 10 (1981):253–264.

Bonoma, T.V.; Zaltman, G.; and Johnston, W.J. *Industrial Buying Behavior.* Report No. 77–117. Cambridge, Mass.: Marketing Science Institute, December 1977.

Bonoma, T.V., and Zaltman, G. *Psychology for Management.* Boston: Kent Publishing Company, 1981.

Boston Consulting Group. "Market Segmentation: The Role of the Industrial Distributor." Boston, Mass., n.d.

Brand, G.T. *The Industrial Buying Decision.* New York: Wiley, 1972.

Brock, T.C. "Communicator-Recipient Similarity and Decision Change." *Journal of Personality and Social Psychology* 1 (June 1965):650–654.

Buzzell, R.D.; Nourse, R.E.M.; Matthews, J.B.; and Levitt, T. *Marketing—A Contemporary Analysis.* New York: McGraw-Hill, 1964, p. 206.

Cardozo, R.N. "Segmenting the Industrial Market." In R.L. King, ed., *Marketing and the New Science of Planning—Fall Conference*

Proceedings, pp. 433–440. Chicago: American Marketing Association, 1968.

Choffray, J.M., and Lilien, G. "A New Approach to Industrial Market Segmentation." *Sloan Management Review* 19 (Spring 1978a):17–30.

———. "Assessing Response to Industrial Marketing Strategy." *Journal of Marketing* 42 (1978b):21–31.

———. "Methodology for Segmenting Industrial Markets on the Basis of Buying Center Composition." Unpublished Working Paper, 1038–79. Massachusetts Institute of Technology, 1979.

Cooley, J.R.; Jackson, D.W.; and Ostrom, L.R. "Analyzing the Relative Power of Participants in Industrial Buying Decisions." In B.A. Greenberg and D.N. Bellenger, eds., *Contemporary Marketing Thought—1977 Educators' Proceedings,* pp. 243–246. Chicago: American Marketing Association, 1977.

Corey, E. Raymond. "Key Options in Market Selection and Product Planning." *Harvard Business Review* (September–October 1975): 119 (HBR Order Number 75502).

———. *Procurement Management: Strategy, Organization, and Decision-Making.* Boston: CBI, 1978a.

———. "Should Companies Centralize Procurement?" *Harvard Business Review* (November–December 1978b):102–110.

Cox, D.F. "Risk Taking and Information Handling in Consumer Behavior." Division of Research, Harvard University, Graduate School of Business Administration, 1967.

Cyert, R.M.; Simon, H.A.; and Trow, D.B. "Observation of a Business Decision." *Journal of Business* 29 (October 1956):237–248.

Delozier, M.W.; Honess, B.; and Morgenroth, W. "Purchasing Behavior and Builder Perceptions of Suppliers in the Construction Industry." Center Paper No. 6. University of South Carolina, November 1974.

Duncan, D.J. "What Motivates Business Buyers." *Harvard Business Review* 18 (Summer 1940): 448–454.

Engel, James F.; Fiorillo, Henry F.; and Cayley, Murray A., eds. *Market Segmentation: Concepts and Applications.* New York: Holt Rinehart and Winston, 1972.

Evans, F.B. "Selling as a Dyadic Relationship—A New Approach." *American Behavioral Scientist* (May 1963):76–79.

"Finding the Real Buying Influences." *Industrial Distribution* (June 1977):33–39.

Frank, Ronald; Massy, William; and Wind, Yoram. *Market Segmentation.* Englewood Cliffs, N.J.: Prentice-Hall, 1972.

French, J.R.P., Jr., and Raven, Bertram. "The Bases of Social Power." In D. Cartwright, ed., *Studies in Social Power*. Ann Arbor: University of Michigan Press, 1959.

Gadel, M.S. "Concentration by Salesmen on Congenial Prospects." *Journal of Marketing* 28 (April 1964):64–66.

Grønhaug, K. "Autonomous vs. Joint Decisions in Organizational Buying." *Industrial Marketing Management* 4 (1975):265–271.

Haas, R. *Industrial Marketing Management*. New York: Petrocelli/Charter, 1976.

Hakansson, H., and Wootz, B. "Supplier Selection in an Industrial Environment—An Experimental Study." *Journal of Marketing Research* 12 (February 1975):46–51.

Haley, R.I. "Benefit Segmentation: A Decision-Oriented Research Tool." *Journal of Marketing* 32 (July 1968):303–315.

Hill, R.M.; Alexander, R.S.; and Cross, J.S. *Industrial Marketing*, 4th ed. Homewood, Ill.: Richard D. Irwin, 1975.

Howard, W.C. "How Industry Buys." Available from Harvard Business School Case Services, Order Number 3-574-083, 1973.

How Industry Buys. New York: Scientific American, 1970.

Johnston, W.J. "Communication Patterns and Influence Networks in Industrial Buying." Ph.D. dissertation, University of Pittsburgh, 1979.

Johnston, W.J., and Bonoma, T.V. "Buying Center Structure and Dynamics." *Journal of Marketing* 45 (Summer 1981):143–156.

Kotter, John P. *Power in Management: How to Understand, Acquire, and Use It*. New York: Amacon, 1979.

Lazo, H. "Emotional Aspects of Industrial Buying." In R.S. Hancock, ed., *Dynamic Marketing for a Changing World—Proceedings of the 43rd National Conference*, pp. 258–265. Chicago: American Marketing Association, 1960.

Levitt, T. "Communications and Industrial Selling." *Journal of Marketing* 31 (1967):15–21.

———. *Marketing for Business Growth*. New York: Wiley, 1974.

Lilien, G.L.; Silk, A.J.; Choffray, J.M.; and Rao, M. "Industrial Advertising Effects and Budgeting Practices." *Journal of Marketing* 40:1 (January 1976):16–24.

Luffman, G.A. "Industrial Buyer Behavior: Some Aspects of the Search Process." *European Journal of Marketing* 8:2 (1975):73–107.

McAleer, G. "Do Industrial Advertisers Understand What Influences Their Markets?" *Journal of Marketing* 38 (January 1974):15–23.

Manville, R. "Why Industrial Companies Must Advertise Their Products." *Industrial Marketing* (October 1978):46–50.

Martilla, J.A. "Word-of-Mouth Communication in the Industrial Adoption Process." *Journal of Marketing Research* (May 1971): 173–178.

Mehrota, S., and Wells, W.D. "Psychographics and Buyer Behavior: Theory and Recent Empirical Findings." In Woodside, Arch; Sheth, J.N.; and Bennett, P.O. (eds.), *Consumer and Industrial Buying Behavior,* pp. 49–68. New York: Elsevier North-Holland, 1977.

Monoky, J.F., Jr.; Mathews, H.Lee; and Wilson, D.T. "Information Source Preference by Industrial Buyers as a Function of the Buying Situation." Working Paper 27. College of Business Administration, Pennsylvania State University, 1975.

Moriarty, Rowland T. "The Use of Organizational Buying Behavior in Assessing Industrial Markets." Ph.D. dissertation, Harvard University Graduate School of Business Administration, 1980.

Parket, R., "The Challenge from Industrial Buyer Perception of Product Non-Differentiation." *Industrial Marketing Management* 2 (June 1973):281–288.

———. "The Effects of Product Perception on Industrial Buyer Behavior." *Industrial Marketing Management* 1 (April 1972): 339–346.

Patchen, M. "The Locus and Basis of Influence on Organizational Decision." *Organizational Behavior and Human Performance* 11 (1974):195–221.

Perreault, W.D., Jr., and Russ, F.A. "Physical Distribution Service in Industrial Purchase Decisions." *Journal of Marketing* 40:2 (April 1976):3–10.

Peters, M.P., and Venkatesan, M. "Exploration of Variables Inherent in Adopting an Industrial Product." *Journal of Marketing Research* 10 (1973):312–315.

Pokempner, S.J. *Information Systems for Sales and Marketing Management.* New York: Conference Board, 1973.

Resnin, A.J.; Turner, P.B.; and Mason, J.B. "Marketers Turn to 'Counter-Segmentation.' " *Harvard Business Review* (September–October 1979):100–106.

de Rijcke, J.G. "Perception of Self versus Others Role in Different Stages of a New Buy Situation: A Survey with Purchasing and Non-Purchasing Executives." *Proceedings.* Conference for Public

Agencies Organizational Buying Behavior, Senanque, France, 1978.

Risley, G. *Modern Industrial Marketing: A Decision-Making Approach*. New York: McGraw-Hill, 1972.

Robinson, P.J.; Faris, C.W.; and Wind, Y. *Industrial Buying and Creative Marketing*. Boston: Allyn and Bacon, 1967.

Schiff, J.S., and Schiff, M. "New Sales Management Tool: ROAM." *Harvard Business Review* 54 (July–August 1976):59–66.

Schiffman, L.G.; Winer, L.; and Graccione, V. "The Role of Mass Communication, Salesmen and Peers in Institutional Buying Decisions." Paper prepared for American Marketing Association Conference, Portland, Oreg., 1974.

Scotton, R.W., and Zallocco, R.L. *Readings in Market Segmentation*. Chicago: American Marketing Association, 1980.

Sheth, J.N. "A Model of Industrial Buying Behavior." *Journal of Marketing* 37 (October 1973):50–56.

Smith, Wendell R. "Product Differentiation and Market Segmentation as Alternative Marketing Strategies." *Journal of Marketing* (July 1956):3–8.

Stephens, H.V. "A Profit-Oriented Marketing Information System." *Management Accounting* (September 1972):37–42.

Strauss, George. "Tactics of Lateral Relationships: The Purchasing Agent." *Administrative Science Quarterly* 7 (September 1962): 161–186.

Tosi, H.L. "The Effects of Expectation Levels and Role Consensus on the Buyer-Seller Dyad." *Journal of Business* 39 (October 1966):516–527.

Walsh, C.E. "Reaching Those 'Hidden' Buying Influences." *Industrial Marketing* (October 1961):164–170.

Webster, F.E., Jr. "Interpersonal Communication and Salesman Effectiveness." *Journal of Marketing* 32 (July 1968a):7–13.

_____. "On the Applicability of Communication Theory to Industrial Markets." *Journal of Marketing Research* 5 (November 1968b).

_____. *Industrial Marketing Strategy*. New York: Wiley, 1979.

_____, and Wind, Yoram. *Organizational Buying Behavior*. Englewood Cliffs, N.J.: Prentice-Hall, 1972.

Weigand, Robert E. "Identifying Industrial Buying Responsibility." *Journal of Marketing Research* (February 1966):81–84.

Wilson, D.T. "Industrial Buyers' Decision-Making Styles." *Journal of Marketing Research* 8 (November 1971):433–436.

————, and Little, B. "Personality and Decision-Making Styles of Purchasing Managers." *Journal of Purchasing* 7:3 (August 1971): 33–40.

Wind, Y., ed. "Special Section: Market Segmentation Research." *Journal of Marketing Research* 15 (August 1978):312–412.

Wind, Y., and Cardozo, R. "Industrial Market Segmentation," *Industrial Marketing Management* 3 (1974):153–166.

Woodside, Arch G.; Sheth, Jagdish N.; and Bennett, Peter D. eds. *Consumer and Industrial Buying Behavior.* New York: Elsevier-North-Holland, 1977.

Index of Names

Index of Subjects

About the Authors

Thomas V. Bonoma is an associate professor at the Graduate School of Business Administration, Harvard University, where he teaches a second-year elective course on marketing implementation in the M.B.A. program. His research interests include both marketing and psychology but center on marketing implementation, industrial buying behavior, and sales management. Some of his more-recent publications are *Industrial Buying Behavior, Executive Survival Manual,* and *Psychology for Management.* His casebook, *Managing Marketing,* will appear in 1984. Professor Bonoma consults to a number of firms on marketing implementation and industrial marketing. He has taught in several executive programs. He received the B.A. from Ohio University, the M.S. from the University of Miami, and the Ph.D. in social psychology from the State University of New York at Albany.

Benson P. Shapiro is the head of the first-year marketing course required for all students in the M.B.A. program at the Graduate School of Business Administration, Harvard University. He previously has been faculty chairman of Strategic Marketing Management, a Harvard program for marketing executives, and has taught sales-management, creative-marketing-strategy, and industrial-marketing courses at Harvard. He also has served as a consultant to more than sixty companies and organizations. Professor Shapiro is the author of *Sales Program Management* (1977) and coauthor of *Problems in Marketing* (1977) and *Marketing Management* (forthcoming). His articles have appeared in journals such as the *Harvard Business Review* and the *Journal of Marketing Research,* and he has edited four *Harvard Business Review* reprint series on sales management, pricing, consumer-product policy, and industrial-product policy. Professor Shapiro received the B.S.E. in chemical engineering from the University of Michigan and the M.B.A. and D.B.A. from Harvard University.